MW00891511

IGNITING CITIES

A Guide to Breaking-Open the
Wells of Revival in Cities, Campuses, & Regions

BY:

MICHAEL THORNTON

Copyright © 2016 by Michael Thornton

Igniting Cities
A Guide to Breaking-Open the Wells of Revival in Cities, Campuses, & Regions
by Michael Thornton

Printed in the United States of America.

ISBN 9781498474191

All rights reserved solely by the author. The author guarantees all contents are orig-inal and do not infringe upon the legal rights of any other person or work. No part of this book may be reproduced in any form without the permission of the author. The views expressed in this book are not necessarily those of the publisher.

Scripture quotations taken from the New International Version (NIV). Copyright © 1973, 1978, 1984, 2011 by Biblica, Inc.™. Used by permission. All rights reserved.

www.xulonpress.com

Introduction

*H*ave you ever wondered why the Azusa Street Revival broke out in California? Why the Welsh Revival was ignited in Wales, England? Is it just a coincidence that these regions were privileged to host God's presence in unusual ways? Or is it possible that God was writing a deeper revival storyline that included the destiny of lands, cities, and regions? We know believers are typically marked to ignite revival and awakening, but what about the land? Can the cities and towns we inhabit be set apart for the same measure of transformation that comes through a heaven sent awakening? Is there a relationship between our identity and the identity of the land we are called to?

Igniting Cities is a book that explores all these possibilities. It is broken down into three major sections which provides a biblical, historical and prophetic framework for topics such as:

- The importance of re-digging wells of revival
- Unlocking the destiny of cities and regions
- Understanding gateway regions
- Re-digging wells vs. breaking them open
- Practical tools in how to open revival wells in a region.
- How our personal identity connects with the land's identity.

If you have a hunger for revival and awakening this book is for you. Although it's primary focus is to unveil heaven's agenda through the land, it gives practical strategies and blue prints for seeing regional transformation. My hope is that by reading its pages, Jesus will ignite a real authentic fire in your heart that leads to the wells of your city being ripped wide open for the King of Kings to enter! Come Lord Jesus!

Dedication

I would like to dedicate this book to a few people. First, I dedicate and offer up this work to Jesus! Before I knew him, I was a committed drug addict who struggled with reading and writing even on the most basic level. He truly has transformed my mind to think freely and clearly. He has given me so much hope and passion to express His heart for revival in America. Thank you Jesus! I would also like to dedicate *Igniting Cities* to all of my family members, close friends, and supporters. Without their sacrifices and encouragement, I most likely would not have finished this book. Lastly, I want to dedicate this book to everyone who has been marked for national and global revival! The hunger burning in your hearts sets my soul on fire!

Contents

Part One: Unlocking the Well's of Heaven

   1. Jesus Loves to Redig Wells of Revival 13
   2. Shechem: The Birthplace of Heaven's
      Government 19
   3. The Government of Fathering 25
   4. The Government of Sonship 33
   5. The Government of the Kingdom 41
   6. The Government of the Spirit 51

Part Two: Unlocking the Well's of America

   7. Carolina: Heaven's Gateway to the South 59
   8. The Revival Womb of the South 69
   9. Massachusetts: Heaven's Gateway to the North 79
  10. The Revival Womb of the North 87

Part Three: The Coming Movement

  11. Two Wombs Are Coining Together 97
  12. The Baptism of Fire: The Coming of
      a New Baptism 107

Appendix:

**A Practical Guide to Breaking Open Wells of Revival
Over Cities and Regions** 117

Part I

Unlocking the Well's of Heaven

Chapter 1:

Jesus Loves to Redig the Wells of Revival

According to the Gospels, Jesus came to earth to do many things. Among them were to "seek and save the lost," "heal the sick," "raise the dead" and "destroy the devil's work" (see Luke 19:10; Mark 2:17; 1 John 3:8). These missions are noble and reveal incredible displays of His nature and His wonder. All are stunning and worthy of our attention. It wasn't until recently, however, that I discovered a powerful secret inside Jesus' ministry.

Hidden in the infamous story of Jesus and the woman at the well (see John 4:4-26), the Gospel of John sheds a marvelous new light on Jesus' earthly ministry. He came to redig the wells of revival. Let me explain.

> Now he [Jesus] had to go through Samaria. So he came to a town in Samaria called Sychar, near the plot of ground Jacob had given to his son Joseph. Jacob's well was there, and Jesus, tired as he was from the journey, sat down by the well (John 4:4-6).

Every time I have approached this story before, my thoughts usually ran to the all-familiar interpretation of Jesus coming to save this wretched woman who was working on her sixth marriage.

But when our ministry began to focus on redigging the revival wells of history I heard that small, still voice whisper an incredible new insight: "I didn't just come to save the woman at the well; I came there to save the well's inheritance." Immediately I knew Jesus was speaking to me about Jacob's well. More important, I was drawn to the small obscure community where the well was located: *Sychar*, the Greek word referring to the town of Shechem.[1]

The Mystery Behind Shechem's Well

To many, Shechem is a mystery. It is rarely discussed or mentioned. Shechem is the place where God led Jacob to establish this historic well and the place where Jesus encountered the woman in the fourth chapter of John. After studying this community for several years, I finally began to grasp the full reason for Jesus' arrival into that obscure city. I saw a bigger picture unfolding. The mystery was unraveling.

I understood that Jesus, the well of heaven, was aligning Himself with a well of the earth in order to unlock the destiny of a region. His very presence in that ancient city began to awaken dry bones, redeem the land and liberate a revival storyline that had been delayed for nearly 1,500 years. I began to understand our identity in Him is divinely connected to the identity of the land to which He has called us.

Moreover, I discovered Jesus' visit to Shechem was intended to finish something rather than start something. "*My food,*" said Jesus, "*is to do the will of him who sent me and to finish his*

---

[1] *Net Bible*, "Sychar." It is available at http://classic.net.bible.org/dictionary. php?word=SYCHAR.

work" (John 4:34). What could there be to finish? To answer this question is to unfold an ancient mystery of why God designates places for pouring out His Spirit.

It Is Time to Uncover the Hidden Wells of Revival in America

Like believers, cities and regions have a destiny too. There history holds the keys for seeing mass releases of revival in America. For many years, however, most of these wells have been sealed and buried. But a moment in history has finally arrived to uncover these hidden wells and ignite them with fire. A hunger is growing among believers today, especially young adults, to know their revival history roots. The bones of the past are beginning to call them into their destiny.

Jesus had a specific reason why He chose to visit Shechem just as He chose to visit Los Angeles for the Azusa Street Revival, New England for the Great Awakening and Wales, England, for the Welsh Revival, and so on. Although these revival movements of the past have produced amazing results, I am convinced that most of them never reached their totality. Differing oppositions have prematurely stopped them.

Many of them are delayed not dead. These wells of revival history are waiting to be broken open again. It is God's heart to "finish" the story not to repeat it. When we redig the wells of our cities, we unlock the destiny within our cities. We find ancient keys that open ancient doors for the King of glory to come in. When this happens, the fire of His presence is ignited on a corporate level, and entire regions burn with a renewed passion for Jesus, and just Jesus!

God has designated certain regions, towns and communities to birth revival movements that can shape history, change culture and host His presence. Still, we have had only a minimal understanding as to why God selects certain places to show up. It is time to connect the dots. Perhaps a deeper meaning exists.

The Purpose of This Book

This book is designed to explore those deeper meanings. It is broken into three major sections. The first deals with unpacking God's progressive plan for the small community of Shechem in the Bible. This will serve as the basis for what I believe God is orchestrating beneath the surface of our nation. Shechem has an amazing revival storyline of which many are unaware. Through these continual encounters this historic city was transformed from a wicked region into a place of opened heavens where revival phenomena became normal. In this section you will also discover how our identity in God is divinely connected to the identity of the land to which He has called us.

The second section reveals the remarkable revival mantle resting on the shoulders of the Carolinas and New England. It will investigate why these locations have been chosen to birth extraordinary revival movements in the past. Furthermore, through Shechem's example, this section of the book will demonstrate how God can summon back to life the bones of revival in a region. Practically, it will encourage you to discover ways you can see your region transformed. Although I am aware of other regions having similar revival history, for this book I have chosen to stick with uncovering these two regions for now. Perhaps at a later date I will write on two more.

The third section ties together what was covered in the previous sections. These chapters are designed to awaken a renewed hunger to break open the revival wells of America. They also communicate God's desire to release another expression of the baptism of fire upon the church. To sum it up, igniting cities is about igniting fresh fire upon dry and barren lands that were once flowing wells of heaven's power. To ignite something means to set it on fire, to cause it to burn. Therefore, the full intention of this book is to set you and the wells of revival resting in your region on fire!

Let's Start Digging

We have approached an hour when Jesus is coming to break open the hidden wells of the past. He is reopening the revival wombs of the South and the wombs of the North to orchestrate perhaps the most significant movement that words cannot yet describe. Insight into what He is doing between these two regions will deepen our understanding of God's plan to reawaken the East Coast and all of America with another wave of revival. And the best part about it is that He has chosen you to complete the task! How exciting! Let's start digging.

Chapter 2:

Shechem: The Birthplace of Heaven's Government

"Abraham is not only promoted, but the region where he encounters God is also promoted."

*M*entioned more than sixty times in the Scriptures, the historic town of Shechem is situated in the geographical center of Israel. During the days of Abraham it was located at the intersection of two major ancient roads that ran directly through Israel. It was the very heart of the Promised Land. Perhaps this is one of the reasons why God would invade this city time after time with different expressions of His presence. In fact, before the mention of Jerusalem, Bethel, Hebron or Jericho, Shechem is recorded in the Bible as being the first place designated to host a divine encounter between Abraham and God. This is huge!

Abram traveled through the land as far as the site of the great tree of Moreh at **Shechem**. At that time the Canaanites were in the land. The Lord **appeared** to Abram and said, *'To your off-spring I will give this land.'* So he built an altar there to the Lord, who had **appeared** to him (Genesis 12:6-7, emphasis mine).

This passage points out that God not only spoke to Abraham, but also "appeared" to him at Shechem. The word "appeared" is the Hebrew word *raah*. It literally means to "become visible" and "to become aware." During this incredible encounter the Lord visibly discloses who He is as a father to Abraham. More important, He makes Abraham aware that the land itself belongs not only to him, but to his future children as well.[2]

The Man and the Land Are Tied Together

As a result of this remarkable experience, Abraham is privileged to become one of the only people in the Old Testament to whom God chooses to reveal Himself as a father. Not since the days of Adam in the garden had God encountered a man as He did with Abraham at Shechem. Interestingly, God selects the unpopular region of Shechem to unfold this.

This reveals that both Abraham and the land where he encounters the Lord are now marked. The destiny of the man and the destiny of the land become intertwined. They are both mantled with an unusual prophetic mandate to birth and govern moves of God. Abraham is not only promoted, but the region where he encounters God is also promoted. Evidence of this is seen through the endless history recorded at Shechem throughout the Scriptures. Here is a list of just a few historic events that emerge from this remote region of the Bible:

- The first place God revealed Himself to Abraham (Genesis 12:1).

- The birthplace of Israel and Christianity (Genesis 12:1; Galatians 3:14).

---

[2] *Strong's Hebrew Concordance 7200*: It is available online at http://biblehub.com/hebrew/7200.htm.

- Jacob and his family lived there (Genesis 33:18).

- Joshua assembled Israel to distribute their inheritance (Joshua 24:1-27).

- Joseph and his brothers are buried there (Acts 7:16).

- Israel divided into the northern and southern kingdoms (1 Kings 12:16).

- Jesus speaks to the Samaritan woman (John 4).

- The Holy Spirit breaks out under Peter and John's ministry (Acts 8:1-25).

In addition, Shechem becomes the womb of Israel and is naturally positioned to be the birthplace of many revivals, reforms and awakenings that occur throughout the entire Bible. In essence, it becomes the spiritual gateway into the rest of Israel. As Shechem goes, so goes the rest of the nation.

Naturally, it becomes a place of "firsts" for the rest of the nation. The passage in Genesis 12:1-7 alone reveals that Shechem is the first place where:

1. Israel's first alter is established.
2. The first sacrifice of the nation is given.
3. The Jewish Nation is born.

Do You Know the Land of Your Anointing?

What is this communicating to us? God calls us to encounter Him at certain places He has already designated. Usually these are those surprise moments where He leads us to a place and makes Himself visible in an area or region where we would least expect it. This is how revival wells are first established in certain locations.

It is His intention to grant us full authority over the regions to which He calls us. Through our encounters with Him we are given access to the lands of our anointing. Our transformation is not only for our benefit, but for the regions' benefit as well. Changed people change cities. Every believer has a land of anointing waiting for him or her to step on. For Abraham and Sarah it was the land of Canaan.

Remember, when the story begins, Sarah's womb is barren. Yet, when her feet touch the land of her anointing, Sarai is transformed to "Sarah," and she becomes impregnated with a nation (Genesis 17:15). Do you know where the land of your anointing is?

As interesting as you might find this, I want to propose a few questions. Why did God choose Shechem as the first place to appear to Abraham and promise all these things? Why not Jerusalem? Why not Bethel? What drew Abraham to this precise location where history would be made? The answer is quite revealing.

Heaven is Governed Through Family

As I pondered why God chose Shechem as the place to birth a nation and personally visit this hero of the faith, I felt extremely stirred to study the origins of the name *Shechem*. Perhaps something was hiding there. What I discovered floored me and opened me up to a whole new level of revelation of why God chose Shechem out of all the other regions within the Promised Land.

In its original Hebrew form, the word *Shechem* is pronounced as *Shek-em'* and literally means "shoulder" or "resting upon shoulders." As soon as I read this, my heart began to burn with the words of Isaiah, stating:

For to us a child is born, to us a son is given, and the **government** will be on his **shoulders** and he will be called Wonderful Counselor, Mighty God, Everlasting Father, Prince of Peace. Of the increase of his government and peace there will be no end (Isaiah 9:6, emphasis mine).

These verses in Isaiah contain several powerful expressions of God mentioned here:

- Everlasting Father as **Father God**

- Prince of Peace as the **Son of God**

- Wonderful Counselor as the **Holy Spirit**

- Mighty God as the **kingdom of God**

It's amazing to see that the government of heaven unfolds through the trinity. That is worth pondering. Before anything existed, the family of God was present in the world existing within the trinity—the Father, Son and Spirit living together in perfect unity expressing themselves in perfect community. Remarkably, it is through the lens of family that we are able to see into how God chooses to govern His kingdom.

Something else worth noting is that the Hebrew word for government means the rule or dominion of God. Surprisingly, out of the many ways God could have chosen to display His power, He found it necessary to do it through the paradigm of a family. In other words, the power of God is released more fully when it is exhibited through a father-son, mother-daughter or brother-sister type of relationship.

Wells Are the Places Where Heaven's Government is Revealed

What does this have to do with Shechem? I pondered this for some time. Then it hit me like a brick wall. God designated Shechem as the place for unraveling the differing expressions of heaven's governing power upon the earth. It is a deep well where the mysteries of the trinity are to be unlocked through those who walk in extraordinary faith. It is a place where explosions of revival are to be birthed. This reveals to us that revival wells are the places where the power of heaven's government is revealed.

This is why God chose to reveal Himself first to Abraham at Shechem, the land of shoulders. It was the place God chose for shouldering heaven's government by becoming the birthing womb of His rule over the land. In prayer about this one day, the Holy Spirit pointed out to me in a whisper, "That's why this story begins in the twelfth chapter of Genesis." Twelve, of course, is the number representing government in the Bible. You just can't make this stuff up!

Over the next few chapters you will discover how God reveals His government through specific encounters at Shechem. From Genesis to the book of Acts are four precise stories where the power of heaven's government is unveiled within this remote community. More specifically, you will learn how God is calling you into a new realm of identity and how you can activate the land to which He has called you.

Chapter 3:

The Government of Fathering

*"The identity God gives you is designed to activate
the inheritance He has promised you."*

*T*he first expression of heaven's rule revealed at Shechem
is the fathering nature of God. Born out of this amazing
encounter at Shechem, Abram undergoes another life-changing
experience five chapters later in Genesis 17. When he is nine-
ty-nine years old, God gives Abram a new identity. He takes him
from the place of being an orphan to the place of being a father.
This is proof that you're never too old to know who you are.

Genesis 17:5 states, *"No longer will you be called Abram;
your name will be Abraham, for I have made you a father of
many nations."* Prior to this name change, Abram meant "exalted
father," but his new name, Abraham, expanded to mean "father
of many nations." This divine identity exchange near Shechem
shows us God empowered Abraham with an unusual type of
spiritual authority to father people. Through his new identity
Abraham now becomes the visible expression of the invisible
"Everlasting Father" on the earth.

As revealing as this is, the buck does not stop here. The
revelation of God as father resting upon Abraham's shoulders
at Shechem has deeper implications. God's plan is not only for

the individual, but also for the land and the people to whom the individual is called. This will make more sense when we discover another secret hiding in the suffix of Abraham's new name, "ham." Watch this!

Uncovering the Root of the Orphan Spirit Over People and Regions

In the days after the great flood Noah and his family were given an opportunity to repopulate the earth. They had a chance for a new beginning. Noah had three sons, Shem, Ham and Japheth, who all had families of their own. One day after getting drunk, Noah passed out naked on the floor. Two of his sons, Shem and Japheth, decided to "cover their father's nakedness" and save him from embarrassment. For reasons not mentioned, their other brother, Ham, did not help his brothers in covering their father, Noah. The Scriptures aren't really clear as to why, but what is clear is Noah's reaction when he awakens (see Genesis 9:18-24).

In anger Noah awakens and places a strong curse of slavery upon Canaan, his grandson, the son of Ham. It is interesting to note that Noah does not curse Ham, but Ham's son Canaan. Canaan was innocent. But the consequences of Ham's actions fell upon Canaan. In other words, as a son, Canaan had to suffer because of his father's mistakes.

What does this imply? Noah cursed sonship! He cursed the ability of Ham and son Canaan to ever have an effective father-son relationship. Adding to that, the curse also drove a wedge between Canaan and his brothers, launching a breeding ground for jealousy, envy and competition to arise among them. "Cursed be Canaan! The lowest of slaves will he be to his brothers," Noah says (Genesis 9: 25). What a low moment for Ham and his son Canaan.

Although this may appear harmless, this single curse from a father placed on Ham's lineage proves to have disastrous effects throughout the Bible. From Ham and Canaan's bloodline comes every one of Israel's enemy nations in the Old Testament, including the Amorites, Canaanites, Jebusites, Hivites, Amalekites, Philistines and many others (see Genesis 10:1-32).

Wars and conflicts between Israel and these nations would bring much bloodshed and difficult times upon the earth. Such transactions authorized curses to fall upon the land. The land became cursed with bareness and drought. Wherever Ham's descendants settled, evidence of these curses followed them, especially in the land they inhabited, the land of Canaan (for curses on the land, see Leviticus 18:25).

From this place, the Canaanite culture evolves into becoming godless and highly immoral. Their mindset is programmed to believe there are no fathers. Fathers are cruel, and since fathers are cruel, all identity and acceptance that should stem from a healthy father-son relationship are broken. Relationships are built on distrust, jealousy and political alliances. Government is promoted through a survival of the fittest type of mentality. Canaan's crowning cities were Sodom and Gomorrah, if that tells you anything. Sound familiar?

Simply put, the curse of Noah becomes the root of what many identify as the orphan spirit or orphan mentality. This type of spiritual slavery leads us to develop a false belief system in our thinking. We believe we are fatherless; no one understands us; we don't fit in anywhere so we begin to strive in our own strength to earn approval and acceptance from others, especially from authoritative figures in our lives. Such a mentality has wounded not only the American culture, but the culture of the church as well. How can this mindset be defeated? Is it even possible to change the entire mindset of a whole city or region?

Only a Father's Love Can Break the Power
of a Father's Curse

Needless to say, when God encountered Abraham at Shechem He did something spectacular. He laid upon Abraham's shoulders the fathering aspect of the trinity and gave him complete authority over Ham, Canaan and the ancient curse Noah had spoken into existence. *"No longer will you be called Abram; your name will be Abra-HAM...."* In essence, Abraham became the father over Ham and the father over Ham's curse (see Genesis 17:5).

Did you catch it? Through his fathering spirit Abra-ham is given power over the orphan spirit resting on Ham, Canaan, Nimrod and every "ite" descendant birthed through their bloodline. The curse hurled from Noah's lips is crushed. The orphan mentality is defeated. Abraham's bones burn with a new authority because of God's promises that *"all the families of the earth will be blessed"* through him (Genesis 12:3). That is, through his new identity as a father in the land.

What are you saying? Only a father's love has the power to break a father's curse. Fathers have an extraordinary ability either to enslave or empower. Words from them can either shape or destroy our true identity. When our fathers curse us, an unbelievable amount of rejection explodes within our hearts. Rejection then is given power over our lives to shape our identity. Self-preservation becomes our new foundation as all of our relationships become limited due to fear of being rejected any further.

On the other hand, when we experience the father's blessing motivated through unconditional love, acceptance is given power to shape our identity. Confidence in who we are explodes. We grow into a new level of self-security. Love becomes our new foundation. Our relationships have no limits on them because we are no longer held in fear of being rejected. Our acceptance in the Father breaks off all limits.

The authority given to Abraham on this spiritual plane is unbelievable. By modeling the Father in heaven, Abraham is given power through his identity to release entire bloodlines of people who are shackled through orphan thinking. By expressing this revelation of God as Father, Abraham's new identity also becomes the foundation for a new nation, Israel. The father and son relational dynamic is restored, making it the primary vehicle for extending heaven's government over the earth.

Chosen by God to birth a spiritual revolution over fatherlessness, Shechem now becomes the starting point for heaven's progressive plan of victory over sin, death, hell and the grave. The story of Israel and the story of Christianity begin here.

Identity Activates Inheritance

Abraham's life shows us we can "take possession" of our inheritance through our identity rather than our ability. It also shows us that the identity God gives us is designed to activate the inheritance He has promised us. Think about it. Abraham was an extraordinary leader. He flowed in the roles of a general and a king. Genesis 14:1-22 reveals that he went to war with five kingdoms over his nephew Lot.

Yet his success as a king or general was not enough for him to unlock his inheritance. These were works he did, titles he fulfilled, offices he held, but it was not who he was. Titles are not evil. In some instances they are needed. But it is our identity, not our titles, that unlocks our inheritance. God marked Abraham's identity as a father. Therefore, the key to unlocking his inheritance over the land depended on his progressive growth into fathering the land versus conquering the land.

It is the trick of the enemy to allure us into thinking what we do overpowers who we are. Satan tried to get Jesus to take a bite of this apple when he tempted Jesus in the desert of Judea. Looking at it from this view, we see only one temptation versus three. The first two serve as set-ups in order to get Jesus to act on the third. Let me put it this way.

Twice, Satan tries to tempt Jesus into performing two miracles out of His own ability. The first two—*"Turn these stones into bread"* and *"throw yourself down"* are performance-based miracles. By tempting Him to perform, the devil promises he would give Jesus His inheritance through the third test: *"If you bow down and worship me, I will give you all kingdoms of the world and their splendor"* (Matthew 4:1-11). What's happening here?

The enemy is trying to get Jesus to reap His inheritance through His ability of doing versus His identity of being. The first two temptations are set-ups to get him to act on the third. The good news is that Satan fails. But it gives you and me discernment into how the enemy tries to hinder us from growing into our identity. Jesus is our example! He models for us that our inheritance can only be unlocked through the identity of who we are versus the ability of what we can do.

Personal Identity Gives Birth to Regional Identity

Abraham's Shechem encounter broke the curse over the whole region of Canaan. The identity of the land itself was liberated. The culture of fathering replaced a culture of fatherlessness. The authority of orphan thinking diminished while the authority of fathering flourished. This shows us that curse's over lands and regions are broken through the power of those who move in identity. Through Abraham's identity as father, God promotes the whole region. He transforms it into a land of covenant rather than a land of curses.

Abraham's personalized identity gives birth to regional identity. His own identity becomes married to the identity of the land to which he is called. His culture of faith replaces their culture of fear. He gives it life. From this point, it is no longer identified as the land of Canaan but the land of promise. To future generations it becomes identified as the land where milk and honey flow. This all points to a marvelous truth: Our personal identity in the Father has power to birth identity to whole regions. Another example of this is found in the life of David.

David's Identity Activates Jerusalem's Destiny

Many would agree that David took on many roles in the Bible. He was a king over a nation, a general over an army and a worshipper over the assembly. A closer look reveals these are things he did, but not who he was. If this is true, then who was he? The Lord gives us insight into his identity in Acts 13:22. This verse exclaims, *"David is a man after my own heart; he will do everything I want him to do."* David's identity was expressed in words by being a man after God's own heart. How awesome is that? Now let's see how his personal identity changes a city.

Through this identity David transforms Jerusalem, the city he is called to govern. After he liberates it from the Jebusites, David chooses Jerusalem as his center to govern the nation. The city itself is renamed the City of David in 2 Samuel 6:16. In essence, Jerusalem now becomes known as a "city after God's own heart" because one man learned how to operate out of his identity rather than his ability. Furthermore, it becomes a city that will do whatever God wants it to do because this was also included in David's identity. What are you saying here?

David's identity from God gave an entire city a new identity. The destiny of the city shifted from being controlled by pagan rulers to a place where the ark of God's presence rested over the nation. Its laws were rewritten. Its culture was changed. The language of twenty-four/seven prayer and worship was born, and it becomes a city that will do everything God wants it to do (see 2 Samuel 6:1-23).

How would you like to see your city become a place that will do all that God wants it to do? Imagine the potential for mass revival and heaven's presence that could break out in every sphere of society. What effect could this have on the education system? How about the local government? Imagine the laws that could be rewritten to promote the welfare of the gospel over the welfare of the enemy.

It is possible! It begins with encountering the Father and allowing Him to author your identity based on His character, not your ability. Such a revelation has the power to transform an entire region. When you learn who you are, you can tell cities who they will become.

Remember: Your identity in God is tied to the identity of the land to which you're called.

Chapter 4:

The Government of Sonship

"Fathers lead us from the place of slavery to freedom,
but sons lead us from the place of freedom to inheritance."

*T*he second expression of heaven's government that unfolds at Shechem is sonship. This is revealed through the life of Moses' spiritual son Joshua. Before Abraham's death the Lord revealed what would happen to his offspring Isaac, Jacob and Jacob's twelve sons. Genesis 15:13 says, *"Know for certain that your descendants will be strangers in a country not their own, and they will be enslaved and mistreated four hundred years."* God goes on to encourage Abraham that in the "fourth generation" his descendants would return to the Promised Land. This prophetic word fully comes to pass when we read about the transition between Moses and Joshua (see Genesis 15:16).

Fathers Lead to Freedom; Sons Lead to Inheritance

Like Abraham, Moses was also a spiritual father. He was charged with the daunting task of leading the million-plus descendants of Abraham back to the Promised Land. His inheritance was not so much in the land as it was with the people he was called to free. One of the highlights of this story unfolds when he leads the Israelites from the chains of Egypt, beyond the Red Sea and into the wilderness of freedom.

This transition reveals a hidden power of spiritual fathers. They possess an ability to bring people from the place of spiritual slavery into glorious freedom. As a fathering figure to Israel, Moses' life fulfilled this part of his mission. The people were free, but now they needed someone to lead them into the land promised to them. They needed someone to lead them into their inheritance.

The Power of Sonship

The first twenty-three chapters of Joshua reveal the explosive conquest of the land. The twenty-fourth chapter reveals something entirely different. A huge shift from conquest to government takes place. Joshua 24:1 opens with the spiritual son of Moses gathering the entire nation to meet at Shechem.

> Then Joshua assembled all the tribes of Israel
> at Shechem. He summoned the elders, leaders,
> judges and officials of Israel, and they presented
> themselves before God.

By this point much had changed since the days of Abraham. No longer were the Israelites just a small group of nomadic families. Through Abraham's leading as a father they had blossomed from a patriarchal form of government into a major nation, a twelve-tribe confederacy state, to be exact. In addition, they needed a centralized location to be established where the laws of God revealed to Moses could find a resting place and govern the people.

It is quite revealing to see at this point God does not raise up another father to fulfill this mission. He raises a son. He raises Joshua to execute Moses' instructions to bring the people into their inheritance. Amazingly, Joshua consummates Moses' mandate at the old well at Shechem, the ancient site where God first appeared to Abraham and made him a father.

Now, four hundred-plus years later, God was reappearing to Abraham's descendants through a son named Joshua. Here, where the very first altar of Israel could still be found, Joshua connects the Israel of old with the Israel of new. Before a word is uttered, Joshua's mere presence at the old well of Shechem fulfills three major prophetic moves of history. Through Joshua's identity as a son, we learn several distinct functions of sonship.

Sonship is Designed to Break Open Prophecy

First, Joshua fulfills an ancient prophetic word that God made to Abraham in Genesis 15:16: "*In the fourth generation your descendants will come back here.*" With the exception of Caleb, Joshua is the only person in that fourth generation to inherit the land. This reveals a unique function of sonship. Sons are given to fulfill prophecy. They bring into the natural what fathers first see in the spiritual. The Scriptures provide other examples of this besides Joshua.

In 1 Kings 13 the "man of God" is stirred to release a powerful prophetic word over the land that is being defiled. Standing boldly in the presence of the wicked king Jeroboam, he states:

> This is what the Lord says: a **son** named Josiah will be born to the house of David. On you he will sacrifice the priests of the high places who now make offerings here, and human bones will be burned on you (1 Kings 13:2, emphasis mine).

Notice the prophecy does not reveal that a king will come, but a son. Josiah did become a king, but his authority to break open this ancient word and redeem the land could only come through his growth into sonship rather than his kingship. Second Chronicles 34 reveals that Josiah breaks open this prophecy near the original site of Shechem several hundred years after it was given.

Perhaps the greatest confirmation of this is seen through Jesus' sonship. Isaiah 53 and Zechariah 9 are burning words hurled from the lips of these prophets into the hearts of Israel. All point to a "son" born of a virgin, who would appear in the earth to redeem both the people and the land. Many years later, while standing in the cool waters of the Jordan River, Jesus steps into His identity as the Son of God. He brings to pass what these fathers have spoken.

The point is this: Those who move in their identity as sons and daughters are given an unusual authority to break open life-altering prophecies over regions. Fathers prophesy the Word, and intercessors pray the Word, but sons break open the Word. They are equipped to lead us in practical ways to "take possession" of the inheritance God has promised to cities and regions.

In this hour, God is breaking open whole cities and regions on a corporate level. He is calling the sons and daughters to their rightful place. They are heaven's response to the longing and groaning of regions that have been locked up. What words and promises of God have been declared over your city? Perhaps God is raising you to fulfill it!

Sonship is Designed to Finish What Fathers Begin

Second, Joshua finished Moses' original mandate from God. Before he died, Moses gave Joshua specific instructions to return to Shechem and establish a centralized location of government for Israel. Moses declares, "*When the Lord your God has brought you into the land you are entering to possess, you are to proclaim on Mount Gerizim the blessings, and on Mount Ebal the curses*" (Deuteronomy 11:29). Mt. Ebal and Mt. Gerizim were two mountain peaks situated close together and separated by a small but beautiful valley, the valley of Shechem.

On these peaks, among the ruins of Abraham's first altar, Joshua establishes the laws and decrees of heaven given to Moses.

Consequently, Shechem becomes this place where sons finish what fathers begin. Here another aspect of the governing nature of sonship is revealed. It teaches us that fathers are called to birth vision, but sons are chosen to carry it out. Fathers have a unique ability to see into heaven, but sons have the ability to bring heaven into the earth.

Equipped with a finishing nature, sons also live to fulfill their father's dreams. As a father to Israelites, Moses' dream was to lead the people into the inheritance of the Promised Land. Yet it was God's intention that the fulfillment of Moses' dream was to be carried out upon the shoulders of his spiritual son, Joshua. A few more examples agree with this.

The relationship between the prophets Elijah and Elisha models this fathering-sonship dynamic. In 1 Kings 19:15-17, toward the end of his ministry, the prophet Elijah is given specific instructions by God to anoint *"Hazel as king over Aram, Jehu as king over Israel, and Elisha as the prophet to succeed Elijah."* But Elijah carries out only one of these requests. He anoints only Elisha and not the two kings. He is taken in that marvelous whirlwind of fire before he can finish the job. The story goes on to reveal that it is Elisha, the son, who finishes Elijah's original mandate of anointing these two kings (see 2 Kings 8:13, 9:1-3).

Here's the deal. Sonship finishes what fathering begins. Elijah's dream was to see the dethronement of his archenemy Jezebel; yet his dream of seeing a liberated Israel was not fully realized until his spiritual son Elisha carries it out. Sonship is the gift that finishes the father's mandate and brings people into their inheritance.

At Shechem it is Joshua who finishes Moses' lifelong dream of entering the Promised Land and establishing God's nation. In this way, sons and daughters become the tangible reality of fathers' dreams.

Sonship Breaks Wells of Revival Open

Third, Joshua fulfills a four-hundred-year-old request from Joseph. In Genesis 50:25, while on his deathbed, Joseph makes a covenant with his brothers that his bones are to be "carried" from Egypt and buried in the Promised Land. Amazingly, the four-hundred-year-old bones of Joseph are carried through the wilderness and into the valley of Shechem. Could you imagine that? They carried a coffin for forty years in the desert. How honoring is that? There is something huge about this!

During the conclusion of Joshua 24, Joshua makes this historic deposit in the land. The Scriptures state:

> And Joseph's bones, which the Israelites had brought up from Egypt, were buried at Shechem in the tract of land that Jacob bought for a hundred pieces of silver from the sons of Hamor, the father of Shechem. This became the inheritance of Joseph's descendants (v. 32).

Wow! By opening the ground and literally ripping up the soil of Shechem, Joshua breaks open an inheritance that had been sealed for centuries. Now not only was Joseph's dream fulfilled, but his family would also inherit the original inheritance God gave them through Jacob.

What does this imply? Sonship releases a power to break open the wells of history. It also reveals that when sons and daughters honor the bones of past revivalists they gain access to their inheritance. In other words, to break open wells of history means to break open the promises of God yet to be fulfilled over our regions. As exciting as this is, there is more to this storyline.

Acts 7:15-16 shows us that not only were Joseph's bones buried at Shechem, but the bones of his eleven brothers were buried there as well. This is amazing! Joseph's story, along with his brother's, culminates when he forgives their unforgivable actions toward him. These actions destroyed their father Jacob and their family. Jealousy, envy and violence ripped them apart for many years. By offering forgiveness to them, Joseph saves their lives and their inheritance.

So why would the Israelites carry Joseph's coffin for forty years in the desert, through the conquest of the land, only to bury his bones in the last chapter of Joshua at Shechem? Let me put it in my words.

Joshua was redeeming the land. By inserting the remains of Joseph and his brothers deep beneath the surface of Shechem, Joshua was expressing to Israel that we are a nation set apart. We are to do business differently from other nations. To validate this, we are prophetically building our storyline upon the bones of forgiveness between our forefathers. No matter what happens to us in the future, whether our children forget the blessings of God or we turn against each other through wars and bloodshed, let it always be remembered that this nation, God's nation, is built upon the foundations of forgiveness and mercy.

When sons open wells, they have an opportunity to reset the course of their history. They open a new chapter.

Prophetically speaking, through this encounter, Shechem also becomes a place where Joshua builds upon the governing rule of fathering established through Abraham, Isaac and Jacob. From this place the beauty of sonship unfolds as Joshua launches a new revelation of government upon the shoulders of a nation. Now, through the demonstration of sonship at Shechem, the people are given complete access to the lands once promised to them.

The Call for Revival Well Breakers

Like Joshua, God is calling forth a new generation of well breakers. So much of the land has been lost to the enemy. Rich wells of revival history have been concealed because our adversary wants to limit our authority and influence in the realms of government, education, business, the church and so on. By breaking open cities and regions where God moved in the past, the inheritance to govern the land on a greater level is restored. We tap into our God-given authority to usher in the kingdom of heaven over the regions to which we are called.

Fathers carry a pioneering authority to dig wells. Sons carry an authority to break them open. They are redeemers of the land and saviors of the inheritance. In their spiritual DNA resides a power to both finish and make history at the same time. They are drawn to the revival wells of history. Regions visited by sweeping revivals in past years await their arrival. The mantles of old find them, and the revival bones of the past pull them into their destiny. Sons do not live to repeat history but to fulfill it. Those who move in sonship will break the wells of history open.

Chapter 5:

The Government of the Kingdom

*"Jesus' DNA is the key to unlocking the government
of the kingdom."*

$\mathcal{A}$nother powerful revelation of heaven's government expressed at Shechem is the kingdom of God. Nearly 1,200 years after Joshua's death, Jesus, the Son of God, comes onto the earth. His arrival signals a new day for Israel and the beginning of Christianity. Prior to His coming, the laws Joshua gave at Shechem to govern Israel had become ineffective. The people broke the agreement they made with God to keep His laws and obey His commands. Curses rather than blessings filled the land. As a result, God promises Israel He will make a new covenant with them. He makes this clear when He says:

> The time is coming, declares the Lord, when I will
> make a new covenant with the house of Israel and
> with the house of Judah. It will not be like the cove-
> nant I made with their forefathers when I took them
> by the hand to lead them out of Egypt, because
> they broke my covenant. . . . This is the covenant
> I will make with the house of Israel after that time,
> declares the Lord. I will put my law in their minds

and write it on their hearts. I will be their God, and
they will be my people (Jeremiah 31:31-33).

This prophecy announces the coming of another type of spiritual government, the kingdom of God. This type of government
is designed to extend heaven's authority within the heart and
mind. It is empowered by conscious living rather than standard-
ized rules and regulations.

The law was given to reveal and restrain sin. It was never
given to save man. It was given to reveal sin to man. Something
else was needed for the redemption of humanity. It is no surprise
God answers by sending the message of the kingdom through
Jesus, who embodies both the son and the father. Let me share
a secret with you about the marvelous kingdom of our God.

Jesus' DNA Is the Key to Unlocking the Power of the Kingdom

Have you ever noticed the difference in the recorded gene-
alogies of Jesus? Out of the four Gospels only two verify Jesus'
ancestry. One is listed in the book of Matthew, the other in the
book of Luke. At first glance, both records of Jesus' ancestors
seem redundant and, at best, boring. A closer look, however,
reveals a powerful secret hiding within the lineage of Jesus'
bloodline. See the chart below.

Matthew 1:2-16	Luke 3:23-38
Abraham was the **father** of Isaac	Jesus was the **son** of Joseph
Isaac the **father** of Jacob	Joseph the **son** of Heli
Jacob the **father** of Judah	The **son** of Matthat
Judah the **father** of Perez	The **son** of Melki
…And so on to Joseph the husband of Mary, of whom was born Jesus.	…And so on to Adam the **son** of God.

According to this, Matthew's account emphasizes the fathering characteristic of Jesus' ancestry. Luke's account, on the other hand, highlights the sonship characteristic of Jesus' ancestry. Matthew stresses the father while Luke stresses the son. Excited by this new discovery, I continued to wrestle with it until I grasped its full meaning. Then it exploded in my heart like a glory bomb.

Jesus carries the DNA of the fathering as well as the DNA of the sonship! In Him heaven's authority to rule as a father is fused with heaven's authority to rule as a son. Arguably, this is the heart and soul of the kingdom.

By its simplest definition, the kingdom of God is the authority or rule of God. How awesome it is to know that Jesus extends heaven's rule through His identity as both the father and the son. Both of these branches of heaven's government rest on His shoulders. His life shows us we can have access to both functions of this divine administration of God's power. Moreover, it shows we can move as fathers in one situation and sons in another. Let's take this a step further.

The Jesus Model

Like Abraham, Jesus models the Father, but in a greater way. He makes this clear to Philip in John's Gospel. Jesus says, *"Believe me when I say that I am in the Father and the Father is in me"* (14:11). Colossians adds, *"He (Jesus) is the image of the invisible God…. For God was pleased to have all his fullness dwell in him* (1:15, 19). Hebrews also echoes this by saying, *"The Son is the radiance of God's glory and the exact representation of his being"* (1:3).

Amazingly, Matthew's genealogy connects Jesus with the fathering inheritance of Abraham. Through His fathering identity Jesus is given power to break curses, heal the orphan mindset, set captives free and overthrow once and for all the government of hell, death and the grave. While He was on earth, the Father indwelt Jesus. He didn't just teach about the Father. He was the Father!

Yet Jesus carries a greater authority than Abraham because He takes fathering to the next level. Paul shows this to us in Galatians 3:14: "*He (Jesus) redeemed us in order that the blessing given to Abraham might come to the Gentiles through Jesus Christ.*" Wow! This is huge! One of the many reasons Jesus died and rose again was so that you and I may inherit what Abraham encountered at Shechem. His resurrection gives us access to attaining our identity and the ability to express the fathering nature of God through our lives. Incredibly, in Jesus, we now have the ability to shoulder heaven's government of fathering.

Jesus, the Son, is also the perfect model of sonship. Everything He did in the Gospels He did from the place of sonship not performance. Rooted in this identity, no jealousy, envy or offense could come close to His heart. Insecurity could not find a home.

Through sonship the self-focused life died to a father-son focused relationship. His ministry did not define Him. His Father did. His own words reveal, "*I tell you the truth, the Son can do nothing by himself; he can only do what he sees the Father doing*" (John 5:19). As a son, Jesus lived to serve and demonstrate the Father. Through sonship Jesus articulates with perfection every characteristic and attribute of who the Father really is.

Jesus Comes to Shechem

Strolling into Shechem, carrying this power of fathering and sonship in His DNA, Jesus made His way to the old well. He had an assignment to finish. He had a well to rip open! The time had come for another explosion of God's government to be established. Through Shechem's prophetic history we now understand that Jesus came not only to save the woman at the well, but to save the well's inheritance. God started something there with Abraham. He built upon it through Joshua. Now Jesus was coming to finish what the Father had begun there thousands of years earlier. What happens next is incredible!

Jesus Awakens the Old Well

Now he (Jesus) had to go through Samaria. So he came to a town in Samaria called Sychar (Shechem), near the plot of ground Jacob had given to his son Joseph. Jacob's well was there, and Jesus, tired as he was from the journey, sat down by the well (John 4:4-6).

While Jesus was sitting at the old well, an unknown Samaritan woman meets Him. A conversation breaks out. This was forbidden, of course, because Jews did not "associate with Samaritans." To the Jews in Jesus' day, Shechem was off limits. It was that neighborhood on the other side of the tracks, if you know what I mean. It is quite possible they even had segregation laws in place to minimize the contact between both people groups (see John 4:9).

As a people, the Jews hated the Samaritans. This stemmed from their racially mixed heritage. Essentially, they were half Jewish and half Gentile. As in the days of Noah, the orphan curse of Ham and Canaan dominated both people groups. Hatred, jealousy and unforgiveness toward one another ruled their thinking.

Although brothers and sisters by blood, they were long-standing enemies by the time Jesus arrives. To make matters more interesting, Jesus engages in a discussion with not just any Samaritan, but rather a Samaritan woman! Little did she know that her life was about to change.

Captured by His presence at the well, this unknown woman was mesmerized by His every word. As the story unfolds, we see her defensive walls come down. His love and mercy melt away the barriers of racial hostility that had long divided their people. Her insecurities fade away in His presence. Something is happening. Underneath the well the ancient bones of forgiveness began to shake the ground as Jesus demonstrates unthinkable mercy toward his Samaritan enemy. Here, at the old well of Shechem, Jesus shows her kindness just as Joseph did to his brothers.

It Takes an Ancient Sound to Break Open an Ancient Well

As Jesus' conversation with the woman deepens, He does the unthinkable. Standing directly on top of Joseph's bones, Jesus unravels another expression of heaven's government, the kingdom. Here He fulfills the rule of the law while ushering in the rule of His Father's kingdom. Next to the old pillar of Joshua and among the ancient ruins of Abraham's first altar, Jesus begins to break open the old well. He declares:

> You Samaritans worship what you do not know; we worship what we do know, for salvation is from the Jews. Yet a time is coming and has now come when the true worshipers will worship the Father in spirit and in truth, for they are the kind of worshipers the Father seeks. God is a Spirit, and his worshipers must worship him in spirit and in truth (John 4:22-24).

By unveiling this revelation, you would think Jesus is uncovering something brand new from heaven, but He is not. In fact, this was an ancient message that carried an ancient sound used to destroy an ancient stronghold. At this very same spot, Joshua gave this same exact message when he confronted national idolatry. Let's go back and read it.

> Now therefore fear the Lord, and serve him in sin-
> cerity and in truth: and put away the gods which
> your fathers served on the other side of the flood,
> and in Egypt; and serve ye the Lord. And if it
> seem evil unto you to serve the Lord, choose you
> this day whom ye will serve; whether the gods
> which your fathers served that were on the other
> side of the flood, or the gods of the Amorites, in
> whose land ye dwell: but as for me and my house,
> we will serve the Lord (Joshua 24:14-15).

Amazingly, the Hebrew words used here for "fear" and "serve" both imply forms of worship. Let's apply it. *"Now therefore worship the Lord, and worship him in sincerity and truth."* Unbelievable! Do you see what's unfolding here? Jesus employs an ancient message through His kingdom identity in order to destroy an ancient stronghold of racial divides between Jews and Samaritans.

Redigging Revelation

We can put it this way. Jesus digs out the revelation of Joshua that had been captured by the enemy throughout the years. This is a major key in breaking open revival wells over historic places. Rediscovering the ancient sounds of worship or messages God highlighted there in years past is very important. Notice that Jesus communicates the same exact message where it was originally given. By redigging the well, He restored the revelation of Joshua that had been lost.

Additionally, Jesus emphasizes worship as being the tip of the shovel. Worship, true vertical worship, uncovers those ancient revelations that have been concealed in our regions by the enemy. King David understood this. In Psalm 24: 7 he wrote, *"Lift up your heads, O you gates, and be lifted up, you ancient doors, that the King of glory may come in."* Notice that

David instructs us that ancient gates are to be "lifted up" and not "opened up."

If gates are to be lifted rather than opened, then how do we lift them? Worship! True worship! When we establish worship at the wells of our city, the gates of our city begin to fly wide open. The king of glory comes to possess them. Crowning revelations of the past are resurrected and baptized with a renewed power. Yet if you're like me, you may be asking a certain question. Why would God choose to use an old message to bring forth revival now?

In revival history, such as the Azusa Street Revival, the Holiness Movement or the Protestant Reformation, hidden revelations of truth come alive to those hungry enough to seek them out. The kicker is that they are never really brand-new revelations, but messages of old expressed through the identities of the emerging generation.

The "baptism with the Holy Spirit" that awakened Azusa Street was as old as the book of Acts. The "justification by faith" message that stirred Martin Luther's heart and triggered the Reformation was as old as Paul when he preached it to the Romans. But many of these remarkable movements ended too soon. The authority behind their revelations faded away. We are left with their words and doctrines, but the demonstrations of their power have dried up.

Love Carries the Movement

If this is true, then how could an old message the woman at the well was probably familiar with change her so quickly? The answer is as simple as it is profound. The difference is love. Love walked back into the original message of Joshua. This resulted in a transformed woman who then transforms her city. Remarkably, through this encounter, Jesus ignites the beginnings of a love revolution between Jews and Samaritans by breathing His love back into an ancient message. This is how God uses revelation from the past to awaken revival in the present.

Additionally, Jesus bestows His government of identity upon the shoulders of the "least of these," an unknown Samaritan woman. By unveiling His identity as the "Messiah" to her, the woman at the well becomes the very first person in Jesus' ministry to know who He really is. Think about it. This is amazing because in Jewish culture she was an outcast. Yet Jesus finds her so worthy that He invites her to become one of the very first recipients to experience His kingdom on earth. Jesus doesn't just reveal Himself to everybody; He reveals Himself to the nobodies!

What does this say to us? Love is strong enough to carry the movements of revival. When love re-enters ancient revelations, ancient powers are awakened. Ancient strongholds over regions are brought down. When this happens, there is a corporate release of regional identity that gives way to a corporate harvest. New tongues of fire begin to communicate new realities of love as the old cultural language of fear and control are burned away.

It also says the crowning messages of old are restored as we dig out ancient sounds once communicated at ancient wells. Out of this place, walls of racism, denominationalism and generational divisions over cities begin to crumble. Opened wells have the power to bring down closed walls!

Another Key in Unlocking Revival Wells over Cities

Additionally, it is the *least of these* that holds the key to unlocking deep wells of the past in our cities. The woman at the well was the key to the city. Through His intentional pursuit of speaking to her, Jesus unlocks her heart. She believes in Him. As a result, the city is unlocked and is thrown into a two-day sweeping revival with Jesus at the center.

This is why the location of the Azusa Street Revival was so powerful. It was adjoined to skid row in Los Angeles. So when the experience of the Holy Spirit baptism exploded, it did so on those living on the streets of skid row; the throwaways, homeless and poor were the ones privileged to encounter that powerful movement. Skid row was a major key in unlocking the city of Los Angeles during this time. The same is true today. When we pursue the least of these at the wells of the past, we will experience new dimensions and realities of the kingdom that have yet to be released.[3]

Remember Jesus was homeless. He said, *"The foxes have holes and the birds have nests, but the Son of Man has nowhere to lay his head"* (Luke 9:58). He identifies with the poor so much because He was homeless for the final three years of His life. A measure of His presence always rests upon the least of these. Yes, worship can bring His presence. Fiery young people and the pure at heart can too. But a special type of presence comes when we connect with the least of these. Isaiah revealed this when he wrote, *"I live in a high and holy place, but also with the one who is contrite and lowly in spirit, to revive the spirit of the lowly and to revive the heart of the contrite"* (57:15).

In these days, God is raising up a new army. A new type of Jesus movement is on the verge of exploding. Only this time, these Jesus people will carry in their spiritual DNA heaven's authority of fathering and sonship. They will have the ability to lead like fathers while moving as sons. They will take people from slavery to freedom and from freedom into inheritance. Their worship will carry a sound that will have the power to break open the wells of the past. Entire cities and campuses will be shifted. Local governments will be impacted and laws changed to promote the gospel.

Remember: It takes an ancient sound to break ancient strong-holds over regions. And it takes a corporate identity to trigger a corporate harvest.

---

[3] Dr. J. Edward Morris and Cindy McCowan, *Azusa Street: They Told Me Their Stories* (UK: Dare2Dream, 2006), 16.

Chapter 6:

The Government of the Holy Spirit

*"Unlock the land and you will unlock the
atmosphere over the land."*

The fourth expression of heaven's government that
explodes at Shechem is the unveiling of the Holy Spirit.
After the initial outpouring of the Holy Spirit in Acts 2 the
spiritual landscape of Jerusalem changed very quickly. As the
church was birthed and expanded, many miraculous signs and
wonders filled the streets. Thousands were saved. Mass salvations and mass deliverances were taking place under the leading
of a family of about 120 followers.

Prior to Acts 2 the disciples were part of individual or isolated displays of power, but after the upper room they moved
into seeing corporate displays of incredible power. They became
the witnesses of not just individual breakthroughs, but regional
and national breakthroughs.

Corporate Explosions of Revival

Amazingly, the first region to experience this corporate
explosion of the Holy Spirit outside Jerusalem was in Samaria.
Although the Bible does not specifically identify the "city" as

Shechem, many scholars such as Matthew Henry and others strongly believe it was. The city of *Sychar* or Shechem was the center of Samaria, and Philip was sent there on a mission.[4] Luke writes:

Philip went down to a city in Samaria and proclaimed the Messiah there. When the crowds heard Philip and saw the signs he performed, they all paid close attention to what he said. For with shrieks, impure spirits came out of many, and many who were paralyzed or lame were healed. So there was great joy in that city (Acts 8:4-17).

Clearly this was a corporate release of power under Philip's arrival in Samaria. Mass salvations, mass healings, miraculous signs and mass water baptisms were all taking place.

In most charismatic circles today this would be defined as revival, but let's be honest. This type of demonstration of the gospel is unusual even in most charismatic practicing churches today. This should provoke us to hunger for more of a corporate release of revival rather within our regions.

As powerful as Philip's visit to Samaria was, something was still missing. Acts gives us more insight:

> When the apostles in Jerusalem heard that Samaria had accepted the word of God, they sent Peter and John to them. When they arrived, they prayed for them that they might receive the Holy Spirit, because the Holy Spirit had not yet come upon any of them; they simply had been baptized into the name of the Lord Jesus. Then Peter and John placed their hands on them, and they received the Holy Spirit (vv. 14-17).

---

[4] "Sychar," *Net Bible*. It is available at http://classic.net.bible.org/dictionary.php?word=SYCHAR.

Did you catch it? Under Philip's leading God gave an extraordinary measure of miracles, salvations, healings and demonic deliverances to confirm the "word." But the Holy Spirit had not yet come! If this measure of miracles and corporate displays of power were occurring under the preaching of the Word, then what happened after the Holy Spirit came?

Unfortunately, the Bible isn't clear as to what happened as a result of the Holy Spirit's arrival. We are left to dream about it. What is clear is that the well of Shechem is revisited yet again. This causes an explosion of revival leading to the expulsion of demonic activity at a corporate level.

This teaches us that cities and regions God has visited in the past; usually carry a greater capacity to "receive" corporate demonstrations of revival. It is often easier to bring people into unity at these places. A great strategy in uniting the church is surfacing historical moves of the past within your region. There is just something special that rests in the DNA of a city that has been visited by God in previous years.

Without knowing it, people respond at a greater level and with a greater hunger to see a greater expression of heaven fall in their midst. At these places it is easier to see church walls and color barriers broken. Amazingly, the history of the past holds a great power in igniting an explosive hunger to see revival in the present.

The Holy Spirit Is Attracted to Opened Wells

When Jesus left Shechem the well had broken loose. The Samaritan people, who had been mistreated and misunderstood, were now awakened to new realities of the kingdom. The bones of Joseph were alive and burning in their hearts. Jesus invited them to rediscover who they were. By valuing them, He gave them their identity back. In doing so, He gave them access to the wells of heaven and eternal life.

This was not the end, but only the means to an end. Jesus' visit to Samaria was only to prepare them for a deeper cleansing of the land itself. We see this when the "word" is first released through Philip. Evil and impure spirits are expelled from the land. They loose their domain as the kingdom, or the "king's domain," fills every home and the city itself. The sound of a "great joy in the city" erupts from the old well (see Acts 8:5-17).

What does this speak to us? The Holy Spirit is attracted to the opened wells of the past. More specifically, He is attracted to corporate releases of joy at old wells. He loves to rest on historical places that have been redeemed and purified by prior moves of God. He loves it when believers are intentional about redeeming cities, campuses and communities that have been defiled by curses, bloodshed and other acts of violence.

An Open Well Is What Opens Heaven

Here lies a great truth. If you unlock the land, you unlock the atmosphere over that land. A deep connection lies between the land and the atmosphere resting over the land. He who controls the region controls the atmosphere over that region. If the land is filled with bloodshed and curses, the atmosphere is closed and seemingly impossible to break through. If the land has been redeemed the atmosphere opens, and it is easier to break through. This paves the way for a greater release of the Holy Spirit to govern the atmosphere of a region. Let's look at it again.

In John 4, Jesus redigs the well by visiting the woman at Shechem. In Acts 8, Philip breaks opens the same well by thundering the name of Jesus. This continual digging of the well gives the Holy Spirit full access to the atmosphere over Samaria by the time Peter and John come. When they arrive, the region is so receptive that it pulls down a corporate release of the Holy Spirit. Extraordinary miracles and unexplainable things occurred. Why? Because the power of an open well collided with the power of an open heaven.

Let me put it like this. This visitation was so great that the well of Shechem, and all of Samaria, becomes this place where the wedding between the Word of God and the Spirit of God is consummated. *"When they heard that Samaria had accepted the word. . .they sent Peter and John that they might receive the Holy Spirit"* (Acts 8:14-15). A similar experience happens in the city of Ephesus when Paul arrives in Acts 19.

The point is this. When the Holy Spirit has charge over the atmosphere, the message has a renewed power behind it. An immeasurable weight fills every letter. It becomes so easy to share the name of Jesus. People flock to altars ready to change their lives. When this occurs, you know the prince of the air is loosing his power and is being blown away by the winds of the Spirit. The sound waves over regions are filled with life and freedom rather than death and restriction. Corporate miracles, blessings and favor overtake ancient curses, defilement and poverty as Jesus is lifted higher than He has ever been in a region.

Many Uncovered Wells Still Remain All over America

Many deep wells remain covered all over America. In this hour God is looking for those who will uncover them and be bold enough to break them open. Dream with God about how you can break open the hidden wells in your region. Ask Jesus for specific approaches and strategies on how to do this. Remember: Opening the wells of revival in your region is the key to opening heaven over your region.

In retrospect, it can be said that Shechem is the birthplace of heaven's government for Israel. It has a mandate to birth movements. But is it possible places exist today with the same effect? Where are the Shechem's of America?

Part II

Unlocking the Wells of America

Chapter 7:

Carolina: Heaven's Gateway to the South

"He who controls the gate controls what comes through the gate."

The Derek Prince Prophecy

On Sunday, April 6, 1975, at Deliverance Tabernacle Temple in Jacksonville, North Carolina, Derek Prince released a powerful prophetic message:

> I have found favor with you here in Eastern North Carolina. I will personally visit you. There will be a revival greater than that of the Great Wales Revival at the turn of the century. There will be kings and leaders that come from the North and South and East and West to study the Eastern North Carolina phenomenon.[5]

---

[5] For more insight into the Derek Prince prophecy see Stephen Everett's *The Sound That Changed Everything: A Prophetic Call Back to the Purposes of God* (Shippensburg, PA: Destiny Image, 2003), chapter 1. For a copy of the Derek Prince prophecy recorded within that meeting in Jacksonville, North Carolina, in 1975, see http://fireinthecarolinas.org/media/prophetic-words/.

What an amazing promise! Amazingly, God is using this powerful prophecy to awaken a sleeping giant. For nearly forty years underground prayer networks all throughout the Carolinas have been travailing for the fulfillment of this historic promise. Such years of consistent prayer have brought much unity between differing churches and age groups.

Why the Carolinas?

One question always drew me to this amazing word preached by Derek Prince. Out of all the states in America, why has God found favor in Eastern North Carolina? Many would agree that North Carolina is some type of a Nazareth among other regions. I am sure many have jokingly said, "What good could come from there?" We are generally known for our sweet tea, warm hospitality and famous Eastern Carolina BBQ, not for being a region where the favor of God rests. But as I began to seek the Lord and peeled back the hidden layers of revival history I was utterly shocked at what I discovered.

To my surprise, I learned that nearly every revival movement that came out of the South began in the Carolinas. In fact, many mainline denominations throughout the southern United States were birthed out of the Tar Heel state. Thousands of Baptist and Methodist congregations can trace their origins to Eastern North Carolina. I found the same to be true for the Pentecostal and charismatic churches of these regions as well.

Like Shechem, the Carolinas have been given a prophetic mandate to birth revival movements. It is a place of firsts for both natural and spiritual phenomenon. As Carolina goes, so goes the South. After learning this, the Derek Prince word over this region began to make perfect sense. God has found favor here in Eastern North Carolina. He does intend to visit this region personally again just as heaven continually revisited Shechem's well. Jesus has an assignment to finish here. Keep reading, and you will discover why He has found favor in the

Carolinas and the coming movement that is about to be birthed through her womb.

From Carolina to California: Unlocking the South

One of the keys to unlocking the inheritance over a region is found in discovering the original boundary lines of that area. God was very specific about this when He informed Joshua concerning their conquest of the land. *"Your territory will extend from the desert to Lebanon, and from the great river, the Euphrates—all the Hittite country—to the Great Sea on the west"* (Joshua 1:4). Knowing the borders of the land to which you are called is critical in understanding how to carry the authority resting upon that land.

God goes on to promise Joshua, *"No one will be able to stand up against you all the days of your life"* (1:5). What's happening? Joshua was giving unlimited authority to rule over his outlined inheritance. Had he tried to cross these lines, the grace to occupy or govern the land would have been lost. He would have been on his own.

Like the boundary lines given to Joshua, the boundary lines of the Carolinas have fallen in pleasant places. Her original layout reveals that the Carolinas were given an unusual amount of authority over the rest of the country. As you will see, the original land grant of the Carolinas was not just limited to the present-day North and South Carolina borders, but rather encompassed all of the southern portions of America, including California.

It is wisdom to know the measure of authority resting upon you as well as the land to which you are called. Discovering these original boundary lines can help you access a greater authority to redeem the land. Moving in this type of grace, you will discover that God will go before you, and you will have unlimited favor and blessing from heaven to support your cause.

In light of this, let us rediscover the Carolinas' ancient boundary lines. I promise you will not be disappointed.

The Carolina Charter 1663

Known as the "Merry Monarch," King Charles II was the king of England, Scotland, France and Ireland in the year 1663. Many years before he was crowned king, however, the English Civil War had devastated much of England. His father, Charles I, was beheaded, and the English Monarchy was replaced with the Oliver Cromwell administration. In 1660 the English restoration began with the rise of Charles II.[6]

To solidify his kingship, Charles II would need a lot of help. He found it in a group of eight wealthy cousins and land barons. In return for their political and financial support, Charles II gave these eight men a large piece of land in the new world known as the Carolinas. Born out of this deal, the Carolina Charter 1663 was formed. Given without limits, King Charles II conferred on these eight lords "absolute power" and full rights to govern the land as they saw fit. The charter went into effect on March 24, 1663.[7]

Although this is a well-known part of North Carolina history, the original boundary lines prescribed by the charter are not. The charter lays out the original Carolina boundary lines by stating:

> And whereas the said Edward Earl of Clarendon, George Duke of Albemarle, William Lord Craven, John Lord Berkley, Anthony Lord Ashley, Sir George Carteret, Sir William Berkley, and Sir John Colleton have humbly besought us to give,

---

[6] Henry Godfrey Rosevear, "Charles II, King of Great Britain and Ireland." *Encyclopedia Britannica*. It is available online at: http://www.britannica.com/biography/Charles-II-king-of-Great-Britain-and-Ireland.

[7] Ibid.

grant and confirm unto them and their heirs, the said country. . .lying and being within our dominions of America, extending from the north end of the island called Lucke island, which lieth in the southern Virginia seas, and within six and thirty degrees of the northern latitude, and to the west as far as the south seas, and so southerly as far as the river St. Matthias, which bordereth upon the coast of Florida, and within one and thirty degrees of northern latitude, and so west in a direct line as far as the south seas aforesaid; together with all and singular ports, harbours, bays, rivers, isles, and islets belonging to the country aforesaid; and also all the soil, lands, fields, woods, mounthills, fields, lakes, rivers, bays and islets.[8]

According to this, the Carolina Charter included not only North and South Carolina, but the entire southern portions of the United States including California. To think places like Alabama, Texas and even Los Angeles were originally under the jurisdiction of Carolina is mind blowing. Nonetheless, because of its unique origins, this charter made the Carolinas the gateway into the rest of the South. Even better, it made the Carolinas the Shechem of the South!

---

[8] *Charter of Carolina, 1663*. Raleigh, North Carolina: North Carolina State Archives. Also see *Original Boundaries of Carolina (1663/1665)*. It is also available online at http://learnnc.org/lp/multimedia/6182.

Carolina: The Gateway to the South

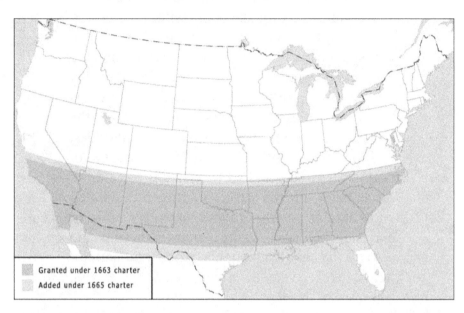

Granted under 1663 charter
Added under 1665 charter

The shaded regions are the original boundary lines of the Carolinas. These boundaries existed for sixty-six years. The Crown of England took it back in 1729 and divided the Carolinas into North and South Carolina (1663-1729).

Like Shechem, the regions of present-day North and South Carolina serve as the open door to the rest of the South. An unusual mantle of influence rests upon her shoulders. It is prophetic in nature and well known in American history as being a place of firsts. Here are some firsts Carolina is known for.[9]

1585: 1ˢᵗ American settlement: Roanoke Lost Colony, Outer Banks, N.C.	**1587:** 1st person born in America: Virginia Dare, Dare County, N.C.
1587: 1st Native American saved and baptized, Chief Manteo, Dare County, N.C.	**1799:** 1st major gold rush in America: Cabarrus County, N.C.

---

[9] For articles on Carolinas' firsts, see *NC Pedia*. Type one of these subjects into the search box in order to find the article. They are all available online at http://ncpedia.org.

1789: 1st university in South: UNC-Chapel Hill, N.C.	**1903:** 1st in flight: the Wright brothers, Kitty Hawk, N.C.
1913: 1st place Babe Ruth hit homerun, Fayetteville, N.C.	**1898:** 1st Coup d'état in American history, Wilmington, N.C.

The War for the Gate

He who controls the gate controls who comes through the gates. As a gateway region, Carolina carries a hefty responsibility. The Bible and revival history are filled with accounts where both the powers of heaven and hell collide at city gates. A deeper look into Shechem's darker side reveals this. Besides being a region where revivals where birthed, it was also a place where great bloodshed, war and betrayal were conceived. Here are some biblical accounts of the spiritual war behind Shechem's gates:

- **Genesis 34:1-31.** Dinah, one of Jacob's daughters, is raped. In revenge Jacob's sons orchestrate a mass murder upon every male in Shechem.

- **Genesis 37:12-24.** Joseph is attacked by his brothers, thrown into a dry well and sold into slavery right outside Shechem. It is quite possible this dry well ends up becoming Jacob's well in John 4, the same well Jesus sits by as He talks with the Samaritan woman.

- **Judges 9:1-6.** Abimelech, one of Gideon's sons, sheds innocent blood by murdering his seventy brothers upon the "stone" at Shechem. Citizens of Shechem then crown him as their leader beside "the great tree and pillar in Shechem." This is the same exact pillar that bore the words of the law engraved by Joshua.

- **1 Kings 12:1-19.** Shechem is the precise location where the kingdom of Israel is ripped in two. Civil war divides the nation as Rehoboam and Jeroboam war for control. Israel is then separated into the Northern (ten tribes) and Southern (two tribes) kingdoms. They remain divided until the invasion of Assyria and Babylon conquer them both.

Like Shechem, Carolina also has a darker side to its gateway legacy. Here are some interesting facts that confirm this:

- **Tuscarora and Yamasee Indian Wars.** The Carolina Charter, when authorized by King Charles II, gave legal right to settlers for the removal of "barbarous people" (Native Americans) from the land. This led to the Tuscarora War of 1712 and the Yamasee War in 1715 where thousands of Natives were killed and their women and children placed into slavery. Both wars occurred within the Carolinas causing much bloodshed over the land.[10]

- **The Birth of Southern Slavery.** The Carolina Charter as a governing document also paved the way for slavery as an institution for the entire South. Between the years 1663-1729 hundreds of thousands of slaves were brought through the Carolina borders. Due to this, the Carolinas became the gateway for Southern slavery to exist in other parts of the nation.[11]

- **Masonic Capitol of the World.** In 1801, Charleston, South Carolina, establishes the Mother Supreme Council

---

[10] Arwin D. Smallwood, *Bertie County:An Eastern Carolina History* (Great Britain: Arcadia Publishers, 2002), 37-53.

[11] *Charter of Carolina, 1663.* Raleigh, North Carolina: North Carolina State Archives.

of the World for Freemasonry. Charleston, whose name was originally Charles-town (named after King Charles II), lies on the thirty-third degree parallel line. The thirty-third degree is the highest degree of Scottish Rite Masonry. This is why the council chose Charleston to hold these secretive meetings.

This organization served as the world's stronghold for the Masonic council and meetings. It was the governing center not only for freemasons in America, but also the entire known world. It remained in Charleston until an extremely rare earthquake devastated the city and demolished the meeting place in 1886. Today it is located in Washington, D.C., and serves as the National Masonic Lodge.[12]

- **The Birth of Jim Crow Laws.** In 1898, Wilmington, North Carolina, erupted with a citywide race riot between the white and black communities. A mob of about 1,500-armed white men opened a hail of gunfire into black neighborhoods. The well-orchestrated assault left hundreds of African-Americans dead. It was the first and only *coup d'état* in American history.

  Better known as an "overthrow of the government," the Wilmington 1898 massacre was an event that stirred national interest. It forced governments all over the South to enforce the brand-new Jim Crow laws of segregation being trumpeted out of *Plessey vs. Ferguson.* Many

---

[12] For an excellent article on this, see *The History of the Ancient and Accepted Scottish Rite of Freemasonry.* It is available online at http://www.nmscottishrite. org/index.php/history-of-the-scottish-rite. Also see James Carter, *History of the Supreme Council, 33: Mother Council of the World Ancient and Accepted Scottish Rite of Freemasonry Southern Jurisdiction, U.S.A. 1861-1891.* It is online at http://www.phoenixmasonry.org/history_of_the_supreme_council_1861-1891. htm.

Southern states implemented the Wilmington's model of brutal tactics of violence into their cities. Within one year every state in the South accepted segregation due to Wilmington's acts of racial violence. Unfortunately, these actions ushered the South into the era of separate but equal. Sadly, North Carolina led the way.[13]

Although this is not an exhaustive list, I think you get the point. Gateway regions, whether they are on a national or localized scale, are going to play a major role in the coming days. The Lord is awakening insight into the importance of our borders. He wants us to understand the scope of authority resting on the lands to which we are called. Why?

He who controls the gate controls what comes through the gate. If the church is in control, then revival will come. If the church is sleeping, then the enemy will take control of the gate. Find the gates of your region, and you will discover how to take back your city!

Lift up your heads, O ye gates; and be ye lift up, ye everlasting doors; and the King of glory shall come in (Psalm 24:7).

---

[13] Michael Thornton, *Fire in the Carolinas: The Revival Legacy of G. B. Cashwell and A. B. Crumpler* (Lake Mary, FL: Creation House, 2014), 102-108.

Chapter 8:

Carolina: The Womb of Revival for the South

*"I am restoring the ancient boundary lines
that have been lost."*

*I*n addition to being a place of firsts among natural things, the Carolinas and more specifically North Carolina are also a place of firsts for spiritual things. It is the womb of revival for the entire South. Here are some significant church movements that exploded first in North Carolina and then spread into different parts of the country.

From Murphy to Manteo: Uncovering the Carolinas' Hidden Wells

- **The Birthplace of the Quaker Movement in the South.** George Fox, the Quaker revivalist and founder, departed from England and traveled to Elizabeth City, North Carolina, in 1672. Fox was one of the first messengers to preach the gospel in Carolina. His meetings led to the formation of the first Quaker meetinghouse in North Carolina. The Carolina Quakers embraced the power of the Holy Spirit and were a powerful movement in the beginning stages. They operated in signs and wonders. They were a revival people. Interestingly, their primary mission was to evangelize the slaves and Indians of the Carolinas. From these initial gatherings around Elizabeth City, Quaker churches began to pop up all over the South.[14]

• **Birthplace of the Baptist Movement for the South**
Following the Quaker movement about fifty-five years later, the Baptist movement broke out about twenty miles east of Elizabeth City. Baptizing hundreds by water, Rev. Paul Palmer came to Shiloh, North Carolina, and preached a series of revival meetings in 1727. With the message of repentance burning in his bones, Palmer's meetings shook the Carolinas. His services produced the very first Baptist church in the entire South. That means every First Baptist, Free-Will Baptist and General Baptist congregation throughout the southern portions of the United States today can trace their roots to Palmer's revivals in Eastern North Carolina.[15]

• **Birthplace of the Moravian Movement for the South**
Coming off the heels of Palmer's baptizing revivals twenty-five years later was Bishop August Spangenberg and a group of radical praying and fasting Moravians. Leaving Bethlehem, Pennsylvania, by foot, they walked straight into the Piedmont sections of North Carolina. Like the Quakers, their mission was to preach the gospel to the Indians and slaves of the South. In many instances,

---

[14] L. Maren Wood, "Quakers." *Learn NC: North Carolina Digital History.* It is available at http://www.learnnc.org/lp/editions/nchist-colonial/1969. Also see George Fox, *Journal of George Fox,* Vol. 1, pp. 216-218.

[15] Preston Heath, Herbert C. Carter, Don Sauls and R. M. Brown, *History of the Pentecostal Free Will Baptist Church Inc.* It is available at http://www.pfwb.org/history.

the Carolina Moravians and Quakers worked together to overthrow the injustice of slavery and the abuse of Native Americans. They set up their headquarters in present-day Winston-Salem, North Carolina. Here these love-burning Moravians established the first revival-based community in the South. From this place, the Carolina Moravians launched a mission movement that brought peace and love among divisions and wars within the Carolinas.[16]

- **Birthplace of the Methodist Movement for the South**
  While researching the Methodist history of the Carolinas, my wife was given a powerful dream by the Lord. In the dream a special package came to her in the mail. It was a beautiful antique doll, dressed in a garment from the colonial period. Also in the dream were a lot of young adults and a powerful worship leader.

As she received the doll, an exuberant rush of sponta-neous worship broke out. On the doll was a banner that displayed the name "Mrs. Currituck, North Carolina." The Lord spoke clearly to us and revealed that the doll symbolized the revival history of the "Carolina Bride" and that He was calling His bride back to her revival roots. Through this dream we began to redig the well of history in Currituck, North Carolina. We were amazed by the Methodist history we found.

On September 28, 1772, Joseph Pilmoor preached the very first Methodist sermon ever heard in the Carolinas. He released this powerful word on the steps of the Currituck County Courthouse in Currituck, North Carolina. Pilmoor, who was sent by John Wesley from

---

[16] Adelaide L. Fries (Editor), *Records of the Moravians in North Carolina*, Vol. 1, 1752-1771, 14-15.

England, was the first Methodist missionary to the Carolinas as well as the South. Even more intriguing was Pilmoor's first message to the South: *"And He will baptize you with the Holy Spirit and fire"* (see Matthew 3:11).

This was the very first Methodist sermon ever preached in this region. Wow! From these burning words Pilmoor gave in North Carolina, Methodism began to shake the ground of this entire region. Amazingly, out of this Matthew 3:11 expression, the first Methodist circuit riders of the South were born. Methodist meeting places began to appear everywhere.

Surprisingly, Methodism's first message to the Carolinas was about Jesus, who baptizes with the Holy Spirit and fire! Remember this was more than one hundred years before the Pentecostal movement would break out in the nation and the Carolinas. Today every Methodist church that exists in the South began with Pilmoor's message at Currituck.[17]

- **Birthplace of Pentecostal Movement in America**
  In 1896, ten years before Azusa Street and five years before the 1901 Topeka, Kansas, Pentecostal outbreak, the North Carolina Cherokee Mountains were rocked with one of the first documented accounts of the Pentecostal experience in America. Cherokee Indians, African-Americans and whites were among the first recipients of this Holy Spirit explosion. It became known as the Shearer Schoolhouse Revival of 1896. During this heavenly visitation people were baptized with the Holy Spirit and spoke in tongues.

---

[17] Margaret C. Pritchard, *History of Pilmoor Memorial Methodist Church, Currituck, NC: Where Methodism Began in North Carolina,* Vol. 1, p. 9.

To date, it is one of the earliest documented accounts of the Holy Spirit baptism with speaking in tongues within the nation. The igniters of this revival were members of a movement called the Fire-Baptized Holiness Church (see chapter 12). Their teachings of the Holy Spirit baptism after the holiness experience directly influenced two future revivalists: Charles F. Parham and William J. Seymour. From this initial gathering in the mountains of North Carolina, the Church of God (Cleveland, Tennessee) was birthed. Today this Pentecostal denomination has grown to more than fifty million believers globally.[18]

- **Birthplace of Southern Pentecostal Movement**
  The wake of the Shearer Schoolhouse meetings in 1896 sent evangelistic shockwaves throughout the Carolinas. They awakened the attention of Rev. G. B. Cashwell, the man destined to become the "Apostle of Pentecost of the South." After the Azusa Street revival began in April 1906, G. B. Cashwell took a six-day train ride to seek his personal Pentecost. After a few days of waiting, Cashwell was baptized with Holy Spirit and spoke in other tongues while seeking in the upstairs room of the Azusa Mission.

  Upon returning from Azusa Street in 1906, he held a powerful Pentecostal meeting in a three-story tobacco prize house in Dunn, North Carolina. For one month the Holy Spirit personally landed in this remote Carolina farming community. Miracles abounded with unusual power. Thousands attended, and the Southern Pentecostal Movement began to take shape. Scholars and church historians now recognize that Cashwell's tobacco house meeting was known as the "Azusa Street of the East Coast."

---

[18] Michael Thornton, *Fire in the Carolinas: The Revival Legacy of G. B. Cashwell and A. B. Crumpler*, 182-183.

It is the only place in America recognized as being another Azusa Street.

Through Cashwell's evangelistic zeal, this revival phenomenon ripped through the entire southern regions of the United States during the turn of the twentieth century. In less than three years, Cashwell spread the Holiness-Pentecostal Movement to more than a dozen states and brought some twelve denominations into the Pentecostal Movement including the Assemblies of God, Church of God (Cleveland, Tennessee), Church of God of Prophecy, International Pentecostal Church of Christ, International Pentecostal Holiness Church, Pentecostal Free Will-Baptist and several others. Today more than seventy million charismatic believers can trace their roots back to Cashwell and the historic meeting that took place at "Azusa East" in rural Dunn, North Carolina.[19]

In addition to these remarkable movements, other powerful ministries, such as those of Derek Prince and Billy Graham, have also come out of the Carolinas. Oral Roberts held his first tent crusade in Durham, North Carolina, and his first pastorate in Fuquay-Varina, North Carolina. Converts won by these powerful revivalists are far too many to count.

Is all of this just coincidence, or is there really something to redigging revival wells? What can we conclude from this? Just as Shechem became the womb of movements that shaped Israel's future, so it is that the Carolinas have become the womb of revival movements that have impacted the entire south.

Today more than one hundred million believers of differing denominations and ethnic groups ranging from Baptist

---

[19] Ibid., 161-165, 167-186.

to charismatic can pinpoint their beginnings in the Carolinas. What an amazing revival legacy this land has been given![20]

Stolen Identity

In sharing this history with others, however, I am often asked why we haven't heard of any of this. This is a question I had too. Unfortunately, most of this revival history in the Carolinas has been neglected due to the South's love affair with slavery. In their beginning, many of these movements did not recognize race or ethnic backgrounds. They touched all classes of people.

The Quakers and Moravians were abolitionists. Ruled by a love for all, they fought tirelessly to end slavery and see revival explode in the hearts of Southern planters and slave owners. Francis Asbury, the first Methodist bishop of America, journeyed to the Carolinas and gave here a strong rebuke. Saying it was the "wickedest place in all of America," Asbury was sickened to his stomach to see how slaves were mistreated in Eastern North Carolina. The pages of his diary are full of agonizing cries against slavery. Often he would bring a black preacher with him when he rode into the South, demonstrating that his gospel was not just limited to the white wealthy landowner but to the landowner's property, the slave, also.[21]

---

[20] I took the present numbers based on each church's history mentioned here. Most were taken from their denominational websites. In adding together the current statistics of these denominations, the one hundred thousand number is an approximate but yet solid figure. This gives us an idea of how impactful these movements still are today.

[21] Francis Asbury, *The Journal and Letters of Francis Asbury,* Vol. 1, 1771-1793 (London: Epworth Press, 1958), 362. The date in Asbury's journal about these events is June 28, 1780. For Asbury's quote about the wickedness of Carolina, see *The News and Observer,* Raleigh, North Carolina, July 3, 1955, 3. This is an excellent article written by Robert King titled "Land of Goshen: How the Gospel Got to Goshen."

The Azusa East revival in Dunn, North Carolina, was no different. Like Azusa Street in Los Angeles, it was built upon black and white experiencing the Holy Spirit together. Even in a time when Jim Crow laws prevented the church from unity, these hungry revivalists refused to segregate. As Frank Bartleman explained at Azusa, "The color line is washed away in the blood." They were overcome with a supernatural love for Jesus and for each other. They spoke the same language. They shared the same mind. Even in persecution they were one.

Yet Southern history reveals to us that racial divisions destroyed much of this unity. In the South today many of these movements remain, but they remain segregated. Whether by generation, race or denomination, the Carolina bride is largely divided. We have forgotten who we are. As a region we have lost our revival identity. We are like the people of Shechem waiting for the day of Jesus' arrival.

As you can see, through these sweeping revivals, the Carolinas were chosen to pioneer heaven's government for the South. We were called to lead by love rather than slavery. We were entrusted to be ruled by the laws of heaven rather than the laws of Jim Crow. But the story doesn't end here. Good news is coming!

Restoring the Ancient Boundaries

Despite the enemy's efforts to conceal these deeply rooted wells, God is in the midst of breaking them back open. After praying into these new discoveries, the Lord began to open up my understanding about the Carolina boundary lines. Pondering the Carolina map, I heard the Lord share this word: "I am restoring the ancient boundary lines that have been lost." Immediately I knew God was somehow restoring the influence the Carolinas once had. I also sensed this would be connected to rediscovering our identity as the gateway to the South.

When Jesus unveiled His kingdom to the woman at the well, He reawakened the destiny of an entire region. He broke off the false ideology that Samaritans were enemies of the Jews and made them one. More important, Jesus restored an entire city's identity. On the surface, Shechem appeared as any other ordinary town, but to God it was very special. It was the location He chose to unravel heaven's government on the earth. He had designed it to be the gateway into the rest of Israel.

By breaking open the old well, Jesus redeemed the influence that Shechem once had during the days of Joshua and Abraham. He restored her boundaries and made her identity clear. Such revelation begs the question, What wells have been concealed in your region? What is the true destiny resting upon your city? The time has come to find hidden wells of the past and break them back open. It is paramount in bringing about the next and final move of God.

Like Shechem, Jesus is reawakening the destiny of the Carolinas. He is redefining who she is. Even after North Carolina became part of the thirteen colonies, it was admitted as the twelfth state in the union. Twelve, of course, represents the number of government in the Bible. You cannot make this stuff up.

As a gateway region, the Carolinas exists to reveal and express God's character throughout the southern United States. She is destined to lead the rest of the South by unfolding heaven's government among her borders. Her shoulders carry an extraordinary mantle to birth fresh revival movements to the nation.

Chapter 9:

Massachusetts: Heaven's Gateway to the North

"God is sending an awakening of revelation of the land itself."

*R*ecently, the Lord began to stir my heart for the northern parts of the East Coast. My focus had primarily been centered on the revival history of the Carolinas and the South. I didn't have a grid for searching out revival wells of the North. I had always been attracted to the Great Awakening and other historic moves around the New England region, but I only had a surface level understanding. Besides, I had never even been to New England. It was the farthest thing from my mind. Then, out of the clear blue, a good friend of mine called and invited me to travel with him to Boston.

Carolina and New England: The Same Revival DNA

I went to Boston to help him plan a future worship event God was leading him to do. He felt the Lord wanted me to go and assist him. Before I could finish praying about it, I knew God wanted me to go. For some reason, I knew God had a purpose for me in Boston. Little did I know that while I was there God would reveal something very important. Surprisingly, I learned the exact same rumblings and stirrings occurring throughout the Carolinas were also happening in New England.

In the Carolinas I had been witnessing surges of revival and awakening occurring through three different fronts: the twenty-four/seven prayer and worship movement, crazy student campus gatherings and the reawakening of certain historical revival cities. After several meetings in the Boston area during this trip, I listened intently as I heard firsthand accounts of how God was moving in New England in three distinct fronts: the twenty-four/seven prayer and worship movement, college campuses and the redigging of revival wells in New England. Completely energized by this, God spoke to my heart while I was there. In my spirit I heard, "Just as I am opening the barren womb of the Carolinas, so I am opening the barren womb of New England."

The North and South Dream

That night when I returned to my hotel room from our meetings I had a profound dream. In the dream I was given a large pair of jeans to wear. Immediately I noticed the pant legs were way too long. The waist fit, but the jeans were a lot longer than my legs. When I awoke the Lord had given me the interpretation.

He revealed that each pant leg represented the revival wells of the North and South. They also symbolized hidden revelation on how the destinies of these two regions were tied together. Like legs, they were designed to walk together. He also showed me why they were longer than my legs. That part of the dream meant this was something we have to grow into.

Let me put it this way. I believe the dream communicates God's agenda to bring these two revival regions together. In history, the North and South have always been separated. Through slavery, the Civil War, the Jim Crow era and even the Mason-Dixon line, these regions have always remained disconnected from each other. Yet something is profound about the thought of these two wombs of revival beginning to turn toward each other. Perhaps this could be a key to unlocking something for the whole East Coast. In light of this dream, I am convinced God is releasing a call to grow deeper into this revelation until the jeans are a perfect fit.

From New England to California: Unlocking the North

After that amazing trip I began to do what I do best, dig. It didn't take long to discover something very exciting. While redigging the history of Massachusetts, I found its history is identical to that of the Carolinas.

Historically, they were very similar in many areas, especially in their original boundary lines. Moreover, I saw a deeper connection forming. I learned that God has laid upon the shoulders of Massachusetts a birthing mantle for revival and awakening movements just like in Carolina. Somehow I knew that by piecing this history together it would serve as a major key in unlocking the destiny over this region.

From this I learned that New England and its heart, Massachusetts, are the gateway to the rest of North America. It is the spiritual gate for the powers of heaven or hell to flow through. As we shall see, everything begins here and progresses to the mid-Atlantic and Midwest portions of the United States.

The Massachusetts Bay Charter 1629

In 1620 a group of radical Puritans boarded the Mayflower and left the shores of England in search of religious freedom. They intended to sail to Virginia, but the winds of providence guided them to the sands of Cape Cod. After they disembarked the ship, they all knelt in prayer thanking God for their journey.

Following this prayer, they moved to Plymouth, Massachusetts, where they established the first English settlement in all of New England as well as the northern part of

America. Within a few years the colony at Plymouth started birthing other communities. Settlements sprang up in Salem, Boston, Cambridge, Lexington and Concord.[22]

On March 4, 1629, King Charles I issued the Massachusetts Bay Charter in order to provide land and government for the explosion of settlers that were funneling into Massachusetts. Like the Carolina Charter, the Massachusetts Bay Charter encompassed a large portion of the United States. Her original boundaries are stated within the charter:

> CHARLES, by the grace of God, King of England, Scotland, France, and Ireland, Defender of the Faith, etc. To all to whom this presents shall come greeting. Whereas, our most dear and royal father, King James, of blessed memory, by his Highness Letters-patents bearing Date at Westminster the third day of November, in the eighteenth Year of His Reign, has given and granted unto the Council established at Plymouth, in the County of Devon, for the planting, ruling, ordering, and governing of New England in America, and to their Successors and Assigns for ever all that Part of America, lying and being in breadth, from **forty degrees of northerly latitude from the equinoctial line, to forty-eight degrees of the said northerly latitude inclusively, and in length, of and within all the breadth aforesaid, throughout the main lands from sea to sea** (emphasis mine).[23]

[22] Earle E. Cairns, *Christianity through the Centuries: A History of the Christian Church* (Grand Rapids, MI: Zondervan, 1996), 359.

[23] *The Charter of Massachusetts Bay 1629*: Compiled and edited under the Act of Congress of June 30, 1906, by Francis Newton Thorpe, Washington, DC: Government Printing Office, 1909. It is available online at http://avalon.law.yale.edu/17th_century/mass03.asp.

According to the charter, Massachusetts originally spanned over five major regions: the New England states, the eastern portions of Canada (including Toronto), most of the mid-Atlantic states, the Midwest states and even the West Coast states. From "sea to sea" meant from the Atlantic to the Pacific.

Amazingly, states like New York, Pennsylvania, Ohio, Illinois, Oregon and even Northern California were originally known as Massachusetts. Furthermore, provinces such as Toronto, Canada, were also known as Massachusetts originally. Below is a map of the extended territory the Massachusetts Charter of 1629 covered.

Massachusetts: The Gateway to the North

With the exception of Virginia, no other state was given a charter like that of Massachusetts or the Carolinas. Remarkably, through the establishment of this royal charter, Massachusetts is the gateway into the rest of the North. A prophetic mantle to birth movements has been placed on her shoulders.

Out of her womb, cities, states, churches and governments all over the northern parts of America were birthed. America's revival storyline began here. Listed below are just a few of the firsts that Massachusetts is known for:

- 1620: First English colony in New England as well as the northern parts of America

- 1621: First Thanksgiving celebrated

- 1634: Boston Common became America's first public park.

- 1636: Harvard, the nation's first university, was founded.

- 1704: The first American newspaper, *The Boston-News Letter,* was published.

- 1780: America's first state constitution was written.

- 1806: The first free African-American church in the U.S. was built in Boston.

- 1928: The first computer was developed in Cambridge.[24]

The King's Highway is another interesting connection between New England and the Carolinas. In 1660 the King's Highway was established as America's first major interstate. The highway began at Boston and traveled more than 1,300 miles along the coast and stopped at Charleston, South Carolina. It was the main road of travel that connected the northern colonies with those in the South. Today, the King's Highway is U.S. Highway 17 and is a major road that runs up and down the

---

[24] For a solid and factual list of Massachusetts's historical firsts, see *Massachusetts Facts Part Four: Miscellaneous Facts.* It is available at http://www.sec.state. ma.us/cis/cismaf/mf4.htm.

East Coast.[25] Below is a map showing how the original King's Highway was laid out.

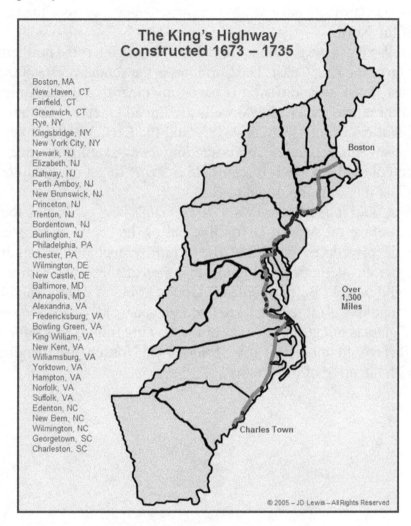

The King's Highway
Constructed 1673 – 1735

Boston, MA
New Haven, CT
Fairfield, CT
Greenwich, CT
Rye, NY
Kingsbridge, NY
New York City, NY
Newark, NJ
Elizabeth, NJ
Rahway, NJ
Perth Amboy, NJ
New Brunswick, NJ
Princeton, NJ
Trenton, NJ
Bordentown, NJ
Burlington, NJ
Philadelphia, PA
Chester, PA
Wilmington, DE
New Castle, DE
Baltimore, MD
Annapolis, MD
Alexandria, VA
Fredericksburg, VA
Bowling Green, VA
King William, VA
New Kent, VA
Williamsburg, VA
Yorktown, VA
Hampton, VA
Norfolk, VA
Suffolk, VA
Edenton, NC
New Bern, NC
Wilmington, NC
Georgetown, SC
Charleston, SC

Boston

Over
1,300
Miles

Charles Town

© 2005 – JD Lewis – All Rights Reserved

Like Shechem and the Carolinas, Massachusetts has been given regional influence over the rest of New England, the

---

[25] J. D. Lewis, *The Royal Colony of South Carolina: The King's Highway*. It is available online at http://www.carolana.com/SC/Royal_Colony/the_kings_highway.html.

mid-Atlantic, the Midwest and even Canada. This region has a calling to birth and bring forth movements from heaven just as the Carolinas have. As Massachusetts goes, so goes the rest of the North.

What can we conclude from this? This region is the northern gate of the East Coast. The Carolinas is the southern gate of the East Coast. In addition, it is becoming clear that the destinies of these two major revival wells are linked together. Although historical events such as slavery and the Civil War have kept these wells separate, God is sending an awakening of revelation of the land itself. It seems He is trying to get our attention about this. It is important to Him.

Could it be that God wants to raise up a new generation that will erase the Mason-Dixon line out of the hearts of people? A deeply rooted wound of racial indifference still exists in America. Perhaps the coming together of these two regions could be the "Balm of Gilead" God is going to use to mend a wound that is more than three hundred years old. Just as the sea of glass is mingled with a sea of fire flowing from God's throne, what would it look like if the bride of the North began merging with the bride of the South?

Chapter 10:

New England: The Womb of Revival Movements

"One breath from the right generation can bring the bones of New England back to life."

With the exception of the Carolinas, perhaps no other region in the United States has been visited, revisited and revived such as New England. Similar to Shechem, this region has been known to be a place where the powers of heaven have invaded its borders. It has an amazing revival storyline.

Many mighty men and women of God have picked up its revival mantle throughout the centuries. Revivalists like Jonathan Edwards, Charles Finney, D. L. Moody, A. J. Gordon, Phoebe Palmer and John Inskip all hail from this region of the United States. Even more exciting is the ability to see how New England's revival story has developed through the rumblings of these powerful revivalists.

Uncovering the Wells of New England

Like the Carolinas, New England is a region that has been impregnated with powerful revival movements of the past. Perhaps this is why it has earned a title as the womb of revival of the North. Check out some of these historic movements that have been birthed through her womb:

- **The Birthplace of the Puritan Movement**Growing out of the Church of England, the Puritan movement exploded throughout Europe during the 1600s. Dissatisfied with the normality and rigid structure of the church, the Puritan revivalists were marked with a spirit of holiness and liberty. The fire of holiness and the desire for godly character resonated deep within their spiritual DNA.

  The Church of England hated them and as a result persecuted many. Undeterred, many of the first settlers came to New England carrying this message of holiness in their bones; hence, the name Puritan. They were a pure people who preached a pure gospel.

  In 1629 a small group of these burning Puritans launched their first congregation in Salem, Massachusetts. From this meeting Puritanism spread like fire. Out of this initial gathering in Salem hundreds of churches began to appear all over New England as well as the mid-Atlantic states of New York, Pennsylvania, Virginia and New Jersey.

  Within just a few years, the Puritan movement directly birthed other revival movements. The Presbyterians, Baptists and even the Quakers all descend from the womb of these early Puritans who met together in Salem, Massachusetts, during 1629. Although this is widely known, what is usually forgotten is that Massachusetts is the region in which they were all born.[26]

---

[26] Eddie L. Hyatt, *America's Revival Heritage: How Christian Reformation and Spiritual Awakening Led to the Formation of the United States of America* (Grapevine, TX: Hyatt Press, 2012), 11-13. Also see Rev. Jeffery Barz-Snell, *A "Short History" of the First Church in Salem.* It is available online at http://firstchurchinsalem.org/long-history-22.html.

- **The Birthplace of the Baptist Movement in America**
  Drawn to the small church meeting in Salem was a
  minister named Roger Williams. A Puritan at heart,
  Williams was a burning preacher who became known
  as the "Father of the Baptists."[27]

  After preaching the gospel in Salem and the Boston
  area first, Williams relocated just across the river and
  planted the very first Baptist church in America during
  1639. It is presently situated in Providence, Rohde Island,
  which used to be under the jurisdiction of Massachusetts.
  Incredibly, every Baptist church in the country began
  right here. Think about that. How many Baptist churches
  are there in New York, Pennsylvania, Ohio or Virginia?

  Today, the global Baptist church holds more than for-
  ty-seven million members and fifty thousand churches
  throughout the country. Astonishingly, the Baptist movement for the entire country was birthed out of the womb
  of New England. Nearly fifty million believers remain
  as the fruit of this powerful movement.[28]

- **The Birthplace of the Quaker Movement**
  Another powerful movement that rocked New England
  was the Quaker movement. Gripped by an "inner light"
  awakening, the Quakers were a revival people who
  moved strongly in the power of the word and spirit. They

---

[27] Richard E. Wentz, *American Religious Traditions: The Shaping of Religion in the United States* (Minneapolis, MN: Fortress Press, 2003), 99-100.

[28] "Roger Williams. . .A Brief Biography," *Roger Williams Family Association*. This is an excellent article on Roger Williams. It is available at http://www. rogerwilliams.org/biography.htm. For a breakdown on the current statistics for the American and global Baptist movement see "Member Body Statistics," Baptist World Alliance, 30 May 2008. It is online at http://www.bwanet.org/about-us2/statistics.

practiced divine healing and believed in demonstrating the gospel through signs and wonders.

Under the leading of George Fox, the Quakers left England and settled first in Boston, Massachusetts, during 1656. Their radical stance on pacifism and separation of church and state separated them even from the Puritans.

Quaker Christopher Holder was one of the first preachers to arise in New England. In 1657 he and a few others planted the very first Quaker meetinghouse in America's history. It was located in Sandwich, Massachusetts. From this gathering Quakerism began to spread rapidly throughout New England and especially into Pennsylvania and New Jersey.

Today the American Quaker church is a small denomination but still holds more than eighty-six thousand members. Their churches are stationed in most of the fifty states. Remarkably, all of them began in Sandwich, Massachusetts, in an underground house meeting.[29]

- **The Birthplace of the First Great Awakening**
  The first and second generation Puritans came to New England and established powerful revival movements reaching out to Native Americans with the gospel. They were hungry and zealous to plant the spirit of revival in the ground. Their grandchildren and great grandchildren, however, lost the original Puritan vision of holy revival. Lust for more land dominated their passions. As tensions between them and Native Americans grew more intense,

---

[29] Jonathan A. Shaw, "A Brief History of Sandwich," *Sandwich Historical Commission*. It is available online at http://sandwichhistory.org/history/. Also see Eddie L. Hyatt, *2000 Years of Charismatic Christianity* (Lake Mary, FL: Charisma House, 2002), 89-92.

wars broke out. The land was filled with bloodshed and the church dead of spiritual fever and life. The need for a spiritual awakening had become great.

Just before a major movement of God is birthed, forerunner rumblings and stirrings often precede it. Under the preaching of Gilbert Tennent and Theodore Frelinghuysen, isolated pockets of revival stirrings began to unfold throughout the Northeast in the 1730s. Then, during the summer of 1735, a preacher named Jonathan Edwards remarked how the "divine presence of God" could be tangibly felt throughout the entire community of Northampton, Massachusetts. The rest is history.[30]

In this atmosphere Edwards began to declare unusual words with unusual power to his congregation. The powers of heaven exploded throughout Northampton, Massachusetts, during the summer of 1735. People were being awakened everywhere.

It was not so much an outpouring or a renewal as it was a "Great Awakening" of the original Puritan vision that had been lost. Their messages were dead, and their revelations had become stale bread. The original vision cast by the first settlers in New England was once bright. According to them, this region was called to be a "city on a hill" and "a bright shining star." The Great Awakening, therefore, breathed a renewed holiness back into the bones of the first Puritans.

Without the use of facebook, instagram or twitter this movement spread like fire. Its biggest impact, however, was felt among three distinct but usually forgotten

---

[30] Eddie Hyatt, *America's Revival Heritage,* 31-34.

fronts: women's place in America, Native Americans and African-American slaves. Amazingly, the minority population of the Northeast was where the greatest surges of the awakening were taking place.

- **The Birthplace of the Student Missions Movement (Mt. Herman 100)**
  In the mid 1800s the college campuses of America began to ache for global evangelization. Sensing this cry among college students, D. L. Moody, the famed evangelist, decided to hold a student gathering in Mt. Herman, Massachusetts, during the summer of 1886. College students showed up from all over.

  The highlight of the conference came when Robert Wilder called a meeting for all those interested in foreign missions. Gripped to see a global missions movement, a hundred students rushed to the front and pledged themselves to become missionaries. The group became known as the Mt. Herman 100.

  Wilder spent the next year circuit-riding 167 college campuses sharing the story of what happened in Mt. Herman, Massachusetts. Students volunteered by the thousands.

  Within just two years five thousand students had answered the call "for global evangelization in one generation." The mantle of D. L. Moody had exploded over these students. The mission fields of the world were suddenly blitzed with young burning kids who preached the simple gospel with power.[31]

---

[31] John R. Mott, *The Student Movement: The History and Organization of the Student Volunteer Movement for Foreign Missions* (August 1889). This amazing article on the Mt. Herman 100 can be accessed at http://www.thetravelingteam. org/articles/the-student-movement.

As the movement continued to spread among campuses, it became known as the Student Volunteer Movement for Foreign Missions (SVM). Some believe the Student Volunteer Movement was one of the greatest mobilization movements in history.

Remarkably, Massachusetts and the New England region birthed this incredible movement that converted entire nations to the gospel. Who knows just how many people groups throughout the world have been won to Jesus through these campus missionaries?

Looking back, the Puritan movement was the first authentic revival movement in America's history. It is the foundation by which the North was laid. Amazingly, a common theme runs through all of these major moves of God from the North. It is holiness. The Puritan, Quaker and Great Awakening movements reveal this.

In light of the current New England culture that has been dominated by liberalism and secularism, it seems these holiness moves are a lost part of history. Like Joseph's bones at Shechem's well, they remain buried and forgotten.

Dry though they may be, all it takes is a spark. One breath from the right generation can bring these dead bones back to life.

Part III

The Coming Movement

Chapter 11:

Two Wombs Are Coming Together

"And as I opened Elizabeth's womb and as I opened Mary's womb, so am I opening up the barren wombs of Carolina and New England."

The Vision of Two Wombs

*J*ust a few years ago I had a profound vision during a conference. While I was there, one of the speakers came over to pray for me. As soon as he touched my head, this 250 lb. man went flying down to the carpet. While I was down on the floor, the Lord gave me an extraordinary vision.

In the vision I was taken to the house of Zachariah and Elizabeth when she was pregnant with John the Baptist. While I was looking at her very pregnant belly, in walked Mary, the mother of Jesus. She was also pregnant with Jesus inside her womb. As Mary entered the house, she greeted Elizabeth with this type of indescribable joy. It was so pure. As soon as that sound filled the house, I saw Elizabeth and Mary's bellies literally tremble and shake uncontrollably with joy and excitement. Then it ended.

When I came to, the Lord shared with me what it meant. This is what I heard the Lord say:

Michael, just as Elizabeth was pregnant with the movement of John, and Mary pregnant with the movement of Jesus, so the Carolinas and New England are pregnant with movements of revival. And as I opened Elizabeth's womb and as I opened Mary's womb, so am I opening up the barren wombs of Carolina and New England. And when these two wombs finally begin to turn toward one another and greet each other, there will be such a trembling and shaking of revival that it will awaken the entire East Coast.

Immediately I understood what God was saying. After you read through this book, I hope you do too. It is clear the Carolinas and New England have an intertwined destiny. As wombs of revival for the nation, they have a major part to play in releasing the next sovereign moves of the Spirit. These lands are pregnant with potential, possibility and power. Their babies are beginning to crown. It is time to push! The question is, what type of movement will God chose to bring through their wombs?

Two Moves Are Joining Together

Historically, two distinct movements came out of the revival wells of the South and the North. Out of Carolina came the message of the baptism with the Holy Spirit and fire. Out of New England came the message of holiness. Both of these movements were powerful in their own ways. According to church history, the Holiness Movement preceded the Pentecostal Movement. From this view, the holiness movement was a John the Baptist type of movement that was given (1800s) to prepare the way for the Pentecostal explosion at Azusa Street (1900s).[32]

---

[32] Michael Thornton, *Fire in the Carolinas*, xi.

Both of these moves have been silent, however, for more than a hundred years in terms of their initial impacts. We are left with their teachings, doctrines and theology, but empty of the corporate releases of power that used to accompany them. Like Shechem, the bones are there, and the well is there; but something is still missing. Jesus has not yet arrived. Thoughts like these have led me to ask questions.

Could it be that God is opening these two revival wombs in order to summon the bones of these ancient revelations back to life? If a person can be "born again," can a revival movement also be born again?

Can there be a rebirthing of holiness and the Holy Spirit baptism in our day? What if it could? Let's explore this a little more.

The Bones of God's Generals Are Beginning to Rattle

William J. Seymour

The Azusa Street Revival was the most powerful account of a corporate revival in America's history. No other records in church history match the level of miracles, signs and wonders that were being displayed during that time (1906-1913). After the miracles dried up and the visible glory cloud faded away from the natural eye, the recognized leader of the movement, William J. Seymour, was given a promise from God. The promise was that in about a hundred years there would be an outpouring of God's Spirit, and His Shekinah glory would return to the church. When this glory returned, it would be greater and farther reaching than what was experienced at Azusa. Many are still contending for the explosion of Seymour's dream of another Azusa.[33]

---

[33] Cindy McCowan and J. Edward Morris, *Azusa Street: They Told Me Their Stories,*133.

Maria Woodworth-Etter

Maria Woodworth-Etter, a powerful revivalist in America, gave a similar word about the coming of the last day revival in July 1913. During a series of revival meetings at Stones Church in Chicago, she declared this to a large audience: "We are not yet up to the fullness of the former rain and that when the latter rain comes, it will far exceed anything we have seen!"[34]

Smith Wigglesworth

In 1947 Smith Wigglesworth unfolded a powerful revelation about a future revival that was revealed to him. It is rare and not well known. Wigglesworth shares that in the coming decades two distinct moves of the Holy Spirit will sweep across the world: "The first move will be characterized by a restoration of the baptism and gifts of the Holy Spirit." He goes on to clarify that this move will lead to a second move that will be classified by the people in that day as "The Great Revival." Wigglesworth says this great revival will explode when "those who emphasize the Word will come together with those who emphasize the Spirit."[35]

John G. Lake

During his later years, John G. Lake preached a series of sermons about the baptism of the Holy Spirit. In them he makes

---

[34] For a great teaching on Marie Woodworth-Etter's "Latter Rain" prophecy, see John Eckhart, *100 Year Old Prophecy*. It is online at http://www.johneckhardtministries.com/orders/100-year-prophecy.html. Also see Michael Edds, *100 Year Old Prophecies Are about to Be Fulfilled*: "The Final Great Awakening: An End-Time Revival." It is online at http://greatawakening.blogspot.com/2012/03/100-year-old-prophecies-of-revival-is.html.

[35] *Smith Wigglesworth's Rare 1947 Prophecy*. A copy of this rare prophecy is featured on "Jonas Clark's Holy Spirit Ministry Training" website. It is found at http://www.jonasclark.com/smith-wigglesworths-rare-1947-prophecy/.

reference to the depths of baptism with the Holy Spirit. He also prophesies the coming of another corporate release of the Spirit baptism upon a new generation—one that would far eclipse his own baptism experience. He even sought for it although he had received his baptism encounter through Azusa Street years prior. Lake writes:

> You dear folks, listen, who are trying to pump up a Pentecost that has worn out years ago. God let it die. There are as many degrees in God in the baptism of the Holy Ghost as there are preachers who preach it. Oh, yes, God baptized me in the Holy Ghost with a wondrous baptism, according to the understanding I possessed ten or fifteen years ago. But I am a candidate today for a new baptism in the Holy Ghost. . .And beloved, one day there are going to be Christians baptized in the Holy Ghost who are away up in the throne of God, away up in the consciousness that is breathed out of His holy heart. And that is the experience that is going to make the sons of God in the world. That is the reason they will take the world for Jesus Christ, and the kingdom will be established, and they will put the crown on the Son of God and declare Him "King of kings and Lord of lords."[36]

Bob Jones

Bob Jones, a well-known prophetic voice to the church in our day, passed away on Valentine's Day, 2014. For decades what he spoke came into existence. Before his passing he had

---

[36] John G. Lake, *The Baptism in the Holy Spirit, Part 2: And some of the things it has produced in my life* (September 1913). You can access this powerful message at http://www.tentmaker.org/holy-spirit/baptism2.htm.

an unusual encounter with the Lord about a coming movement of holiness and the baptism of fire that would explode all
over the earth. Bob's wife, Bonnie, shares about her husband's
experience:

> Bob was handed a huge white egg, and as it was
> placed in his hand it began to hatch open. As he
> drew closer to examine the egg, he saw that it
> had fire inside and it was like a birthing of fire.
> This egg represents a new birthing and new life
> because it represents the second birthing of the
> baptism of fire. This baptism will be far greater
> than Pentecost and more powerful than Azusa
> Street of recent times. I believe we're all getting
> ready to be birthed a second time in fire . . .this
> baptism of fire means that plagues and viruses
> cannot cling to it. No demonic control can sur-
> vive around it, and the enemy cannot trouble you.
> The baptism of fire will bring in holiness . . .God
> is a holy God, and when we are consumed by this
> baptism of fire, anything unholy that comes into
> our presence will not be able to stand. The power
> of this consuming fire will cause demons to flee
> and sickness, disease, infirmities and plagues to
> die instantly. There will be no question that the
> power of God is resident in His people.[37]

Take Note

Did you take note of a similar message being communicated through these mighty men and women of God? Most of
them share a common theme. They speak of a rebirthing or

---

[37] Bob Jones, *Baptism of Fire: Second Birthing*. This article is online at http://www.
bobjones.org/Docs/Words%20of%202013/2013-10_BaptismOfFire.htm.

restoration of holiness and the baptism with the Holy Spirit as a hallmark of this coming move of God. This is interesting.

Decades ago, the baptism with the Holy Spirit was considered a very controversial and taboo topic within the church. It was very divisive. Many pastors and teachers have opted to stay away from it. It is true that in past years Pentecostals/ Charismatic's have abused and manipulated this wonderful experience. As a believer in this baptism experience, I offer my sincere and deepest apologies. Remember: Jesus intended it to be the gift of God, not the curse of God.

Despite the flaws of this history, a constant growing hunger still remains in this generation to both know and experience the baptism with the Holy Spirit and fire. They have a natural craving in their DNA for more of God. They want the God of the Bible. They want to go deeper with the Lord. They crave to walk in the supernatural. Many just don't know how to express it. They are even unsure of how to approach God to ask for more. The language is not there yet, and that's okay. Let me help by sharing some of my story.

Hunger for More: My experience

Every revival in church history, every God-inspired movement that has shaped history, begins at the place of renewed hunger for more. Hunger is a gift. Layers are associated with it and can be a powerful catalyst for change. Let me share with you some highlights of my own experience of going after more of God. I hope it creates hunger for more of Him in your life.

Before I was saved I was hopelessly addicted to crack-cocaine for ten years. At my lowest, I prostituted my body for drugs. Homeless and completely broken, I finally hungered for God to save my life. He answered me by filling me with the joys of salvation and renewed life. His consuming love broke every form of addiction and unbelief in my life. I felt His presence, His love. I experienced the Holy Spirit. I spoke in tongues and began to grow in the spiritual gifts. Everything was new, and everything changed. I have been free from addictions of every kind ever since that time. In addition, the Lord has blessed me with a beautiful wife and five amazing children. I have learned to become a very thankful and blessed man.

Nearly twelve years later, however, I hunger for more. Although I am satisfied, I have an undeniable hunger deep in my soul for more of Him. It is true. I have encountered the baptism of the Holy Spirit, or at least according to our current understanding of it. Our family has been engaged in full-time ministry for many years and has witnessed many supernatural miracles, salvations and healings of bodies. Still, when I read stories of Azusa Street or in the book of Acts, my baptism experience seems to fall way short.

Rather than sinking into a spiritual depression, the Azusa stories and the book of Acts have only provoked my need for more of God to invade my bones. I have hope there is more. But my hunger is not just to get a word. It's not just a hunger to provide an answer or solution to a problem. My hunger is for my life to be changed yet again. This pursuit has led me to seek a rebirthing of the baptism of fire. Theologically, that has presented some challenges. But my current questions are beginning to drown out my previous views. My hunger for God is finally overtaking my fear of failure. I am ready for more. How about you?

Let's Get Practical: Heart-Searching Questions

In light of this, how can two revival wombs such as the Carolinas and New England join together? What does that look like? How can it be walked out? Honestly, I am not sure if I have the answer. My hope is that this book is igniting a deep hunger in you to take this further.

I do sense, however, that a major key in seeing these two regions join together is found in breaking open their historic wells of revival history. I feel the Lord is opening the barren wombs of revival all over the country, not just in the North and South. This is only an example of something Jesus is doing all over the nation. When these wells, regions or gates begin to explore ways to encourage and bless one another on purpose, something powerful is going to be released.

Let Jesus and His relationship with the well of Shechem become our example. While there, He breathed life into an ancient message that caused dry bones to live again and brought Jews and Samaritans together. He plugged Samaria back into the storyline of Israel. He snatched their region from the place of fear and plugged them back into the realm of faith. Why can't He do the same today?

Although this may point us in an uncomfortable direction, here are a few heart-searching questions I would like to address. They will prepare us for the next and final chapter. Is there another definite and distinct baptism experience beyond the baptism with the Holy Spirit? If so, is it in Scripture, and has it ever been released yet?

Chapter 12:

The Fire: The Coming of a New Baptism

*"I released the baptism with the Holy Spirit to **birth** my church; but now I am going to release the baptism of fire to **harvest** my church."*

An Encounter with Jesus, the King of Fire

In January 2014 I had a life-changing encounter. While taking part in a young adult gathering called the Launch, I was overcome by a vision of Jesus Himself. As worship began, the presence of God saturated the large auditorium. While singing "Hosanna in the highest," I saw Jesus appear in the room. He was wearing a bright white garment with a purple sash draped around His chest. On His head He wore a special crown. It was a crown of olive leaves and branches. As soon as I began to ponder what I was beholding, the vision shifted. Worship moved from "Hosanna in the highest" to "baptize me with fire." Jesus also moved. He moved from being the Prince of Peace to being the King of fire.

Standing directly in front of me, Jesus was staring me down while His entire being was consumed in fire. My jaw dropped. It was so real, so clear. His crown, which was now made of pure gold and studded with diamonds, was completely on fire. His eyes were fire, His beard burning with heavenly flames. His tongue was a tongue of fire, His lips and mouth both consumed in a blaze of dazzling light. He held up His hands and showed me the holes left from the nail marks.

As soon as I looked through them, flames flew out. Paralyzed in awe, Jesus, the King of fire, reached out His hand and touched me. He touched my eyes, my lips and then my heart. Backing up, Jesus gazed into my eyes and offered me a challenge. He said to me, "Now come and step into My fire." As quickly as it began, it ended.

A Different Baptism

Growing out of this fiery encounter, I had a renewed passion to seek Jesus even more. After spending time in the Word and in contemplative prayer over this experience, the Lord began to reveal the purpose of this unusual experience. To my surprise, it is connected to a harvesting movement of holy fire that God desires to birth through the revival wells of America. While in prayer I heard this:

> There is coming, My son, a fresh baptism of fire, My holy fire, which will begin to ignite and explode all around the world. This fire will be all consuming. It will consume all sin and will refine and purify My bride. Michael, the coming baptism of fire is not the end result. The power resting in My fire is an aspect of My nature that has been hidden until this "day," this season. And when you and your generation begin to step into the fire and are consumed, the harvest of the ages shall commence!

Following this, I began to understand this wasn't going to be a "flash in the pan" or just some heightened emotional experience. I also understood this was something people have not collectively or corporately experienced yet, including the current population of charismatic/Pentecostal believers. This baptism of fire is going to be a sovereign movement of God separate and distinct from the baptism of the Holy Spirit.

Has This Ever Happened Before in Revival History?

In 1895 a young Holiness preacher, Benjamin Harden Irwin, had a life-changing encounter in Lincoln, Nebraska. He wrote about it in a nationally recognized religious newspaper titled *The Way of Faith*. In this vivid account B. H. Irwin shares about his experience with the "FIRE" which, according to him, came after the baptism with the Holy Spirit. Irwin writes:

> While I knew and enjoyed the experience of entire sanctification (holiness) and had the baptism of the Holy Ghost upon my soul, yet I knew that some of the brethren enjoyed an experience of fire unknown to me. . .God sent Bro. C. P. Carkuff two hundred and fifty miles, all the way from Ness City, Kansas, to tell me his experience, and while he was relating it to me, about 12 o'clock in the night, of the 23rd of October, 1895. . .I saw in the room above me a cross of pure transparent fire. It was all fire. The very walls of the room seemed to be on fire. My entire being, spirit, soul and body, seemed literally conflagrant. It is not a cleansing; it is not the witness of the Spirit; it is not the baptism with the Holy Ghost; it is not

a dream; it is not a delusion or a deception; it is none of these. It is the baptism of fire.[38]

As Irwin shared this experience, the baptism of fire exploded in the Midwest and took root in my heart. In one year, fire-baptized meeting places were found in Iowa, Kansas, Oklahoma and Texas. This movement became known as the Fire-Baptized Holiness Association.

Sadly, within just a few years of its beginning, this movement suffered a tremendous blow due to Irwin undergoing a moral failure. Due to this, and other fanatical teachings that crept in, the baptism of fire experience came under severe attack. This is one of many reasons why this has been generally unknown to the public. The movement later became absorbed in the Pentecostal movement after the Azusa Street Revival in 1906.

Looking back, I think B. H. Irwin had a genuine experience with the baptism of fire. His hunger for more gave him access to something beyond his times. Both he and his leaders may have not been quite ready to carry the weight of this revelation as a separate and distinct movement. This is a huge lesson for us today. Nonetheless, B. H. Irwin's impacts are undeniable and made a strong impression on rising leaders of Azusa Street.

Think about it this way. B. H. Irwin's baptism of fire account occurred eleven years before Azusa Street and six years before the Topeka outbreak of Pentecost in 1901. In fact, it was Irwin's teachings that directly influenced Charles F. Parham to open a Bible school for students hungry to receive an experience beyond holiness. One of those students was William J. Seymour, who was called to ignite the Azusa Street Revival and restore the baptism with the Holy Spirit to the global church.

Now, 120 years later, perhaps we are finally ready for another wave of the fire baptism. Is it possible God is going to release this renewed baptism of fire to our generation? Just maybe we

---

[38] B. H. Irwin, "The Baptism of Fire," *The Way of Faith*, November 13, 1895.

are that people John G. Lake prophesied about—the generation that would fully mature into their identity as sons and daughters before it comes. That generation, Lake says, would become candidates to receive a higher measure of the Spirit's baptism than he or his peers at Azusa ever received.

The Fire Is unto the Final Harvest

As I wrestled with these historical accounts and my present encounter, God began to unfold this revelation a little more. I heard the small still voice whisper, "I released the baptism with the Holy Spirit to **birth** my church; but now I am going to release the baptism of fire to **harvest** my church." Wow! Suddenly everything made sense. Jesus, the baptizer, doesn't come with only one baptism; He comes with two (see Matthew 3:11; Luke 3:16; Luke 12:50).

This baptism of Jesus' own fire will not be unto another doctrine. It will not be unto another church or denomination. This baptism of fire will be unto the harvest, a billion- plus soul harvest. Jesus gave insight into this final revival through the tares and wheat story. Jesus made it clear the last revival movement of history will be a harvesting type of movement.

> The **harvest is the end of the age**, and the **harvesters are angels.** As the weeds are pulled up and **burned in the fire, so it will be at the end of the age** . . .the Son of Man will send out his angels, and they will weed out of his kingdom everything that causes sin and all who do evil (Matthew 13:39, 41 emphasis mine).

The greatest harvest in history is about to explode. Heaven's armies are coming to invade earth's wells. Jesus is sending a flood of angels to be the last day harvesters. This is going to be on a level we have never seen before. The ancient gates for unprecedented revival are opening again.

Unexpected Fire Will Explode in Unexpected Places

In the days to come, regions marked by old revivals will begin to see heightened angelic activity. Explosions of dreams and visions will spill over in these places. Angelic encounters will be on the rise. In these gateway regions, look for the homeless missions, the halfway houses and the soup-kitchen-type places to be transformed into houses of fire that release waves of creative miracles. Look for the nameless and faceless women at the wells. Search out those places where the church has been hesitant to go. There, God will be moving.

Jesus is going to show up in the most unlikely places. Keep watch on the marketplaces. This fire is going to consume the consumers of business and trade. Look for the youth and young-adult meeting places to explode with unexplainable miracles. The face of schools and campuses will change into love-burning centers, as the bones of the past will suddenly come to life. Unexpected fire is going to burn in unexpected places. And it will burn the brightest in unexpected hearts.

Although many regions are being awakened for this, the Carolinas and New England will be major birthing centers for this harvesting movement. Just as the Holy Spirit had impregnated Mary and broke Elizabeth's barrenness with movements of heaven, He is impregnating these unexpected places with a movement of His fire. This baptism is going to become a key that unlocks all the other hidden wells in the country. Jesus is on the move, and He is coming to the Shechem's of America to set their bones on fire.

The Baptism of Fire Is the Expression of Jesus

The baptism of fire is an expression of Jesus Himself. He is the center. Surprisingly, the very first and last announcement of His ministry in the New Testament confirms this. Matthew 3:11 reveals, *"He (Jesus) will baptize you with the Holy Spirit and fire."* In the final moment before Jesus is taken to heaven after the forty days of His resurrection, He says this: *"For John baptized with water, but in a few days you will be baptized with the Holy Spirit . . . After he said this, he was taken up before their very eyes"* (Acts 1:5, 9). This is something worth noting because in properly interpreting Scripture, when something is first introduced or finalized in the Bible, it carries a lot of weight in terms of revelation.

Here is something else to note as well. In the Acts 1:5 passage, Jesus informs His disciples they will be baptized with the Holy Spirit, but not with the fire. Their baptism was fulfilled in the upper room. Tongues of fire came to rest on them. The fire illuminated just one gift out of nine (tongues), and the church was birthed.

What if this baptism of fire comes to illuminate all nine of those gifts simultaneously instead of just one? Imagine all the gifts of His Spirit operating at full capacity because of the explosion of a love the church has not yet grasped. In 1 Corinthians 13, Paul makes it clear that when love is absent our gifts operate at an imperfect and immature level. They work, but they have no power in them. In this context, though, Paul also said when the *"perfection comes, the imperfect disappears."* Just what if the imperfect mentioned here is not the canonized Bible, but the release of a baptism of fiery love that has the ability to flush all impurities and immaturity out of the spiritual gifts of the church?

The Baptism of Fire As an Experience

In recent years a hunger to see an explosion of revival fire has been growing in the Carolina and New England regions. Cities and college campuses are being filled with young people who are giving themselves over to night and day prayer, united fasting and corporate evangelism. The old model of church is dying, and a new model is forming. All are like spiritual birth pains, leading to something greater. All point to a youth-led harvesting movement of fire that will burn with Jesus at its center. But what will this fiery Jesus movement look like?

The baptism of fire, as personalized experience, is coming to burn away everything in us that is not like Him. If something is hiding in our nature, character or even our personality, the fire is coming to set it ablaze. It is designed not only to burn away sin on the surface, but also to burn away those things that cause sin (see Matthew 13:41; Malachi 4:1). Anything hindering His church from expressing the beauty and wonder of His image will be consumed. One of the crowning purposes of this fire will be to become more like Jesus in everything we say or do.

In addition to the burning away of sin personally and corporately, the baptism of fire will illuminate and make bright the very nature, character and personality of Jesus within His body. Through His church He will set His own love on fire, with His meekness and humility burning through the lives yielded to His personal desires. His compassion for the lost set a blaze through the local assembly.

The prophet Malachi was given a glimpse into this movement. "*Surely the day is coming; it will burn like a furnace. All the arrogant and every evildoer will be stubble, and that day that is coming will set them on fire*" (4:1). The word "day" used here in Hebrew is rendered as *yom*, which means an age or extended period of time. It is not a twenty-four-hour period, but rather a specific season that is coming upon the earth. It speaks of a time and a season of God's fire that will appear on the earth. It reveals that not just people will burn for Him, but the ground, environment and atmosphere will also be consumed in His fiery presence.

The Baptism of Fire As a Movement

Out of this fresh release of fire, I believe leading voices are going to emerge throughout the nation. Even now God is raising up ordinary people to become last-day messengers of His fire. Their calling will not be to vocational ministry as in the past. Their calling will be to express the very nature of Christ, to release an ever-increasing measure of Jesus' own burning love to a loveless generation.

The marketplace will explode with unusual revival-type phenomenon like Ephesus in the days of Acts. Local government chambers will become expressions of heaven's government. They will impart the consuming fire of God's humility into cultures built on pride.

With eyes like burning torches, these fiery ones will open a greater vision of who Jesus is to the body of Christ. With tongues of fire, they will communicate pure messages from the throne room of heaven. With burning hearts, love for Jesus and love for people will consume their every desire. Their meetings will be filled with awe and wonder.

I see days coming when, without the help of words or music, the fire of His presence will ignite the atmosphere. Angels will break in to work the altars. Explosions of new sounds and new songs will fill city streets. Stadiums will resound with unprecedented gatherings of ordinary people taking back their cities. The sick and the dying will be brought there. All forms of sicknesses and incurable diseases will vanish. The fire in the air will consume them without even the help of prayers or hands laid on. Jesus will get all the glory! Whole cities will be transformed. Entire campuses will be consumed with burning passion for Jesus, and just Jesus!

In corporate settings hundreds of people will corporately experience the baptism of fire instantaneously. It will be a quick work. They will burn like they never burned before. The church as we know it will change as we transition into a new era of harvest. Although this fire movement is destined to break out all over the earth, God is opening the barren wombs of Carolina and New England to help birth it.

Closing Thoughts . . .

Traditionally, we have been taught to believe the baptism with the Holy Spirit and fire are one and the same, but what if it isn't? What if the two are separate and distinct from each other? What if it has been withheld until this time? The Bible does not place a numerical limit on how many times believers can be baptized or filled with the Holy Spirit or the fire. I have resolved that if it takes one hundred baptisms to make me more like Jesus, then I desire to undergo them all. How about you?

Appendix

A Practical Guide to Breaking Open Wells of Revival over Cities and Regions

Redigging the Well vs. Reopening the Well

*I*n the book of Genesis we find a fascinating story about Isaac redigging and reopening the wells of his father Abraham.

> So all the wells that his father's servants had dug in the time of his father Abraham, the Philistines stopped up, filling them with earth . . .Isaac digged again the wells that had been dug in the time of his father Abraham (26:15, 18).

A deeper look into this passage reveals something very interesting. The word for "digged," as used here, is the Hebrew word *chaphar* and literally means to search for. In other words, in ancient times, to redig a well was to first locate it. Once located, the wells underwent a digging-out process. In Isaac's case, the wells were "hidden" by the enemy. The Philistines had completely covered them up with mud and dirt. So the process of redigging wells began with locating it first, cleaning the well out then breaking it back open to release fresh water.

To sum it up, redigging wells has three steps to it: 1) locate the well; 2) dig out the well; and 3) break it open again with flowing and living water. In light of this, I would like to share with you some practical ways that will help you redig and ignite the wells hiding in your regions.

1. Locating the Wells: Spiritual Mapping of Your City, Campus and Region

7 Ways to Locate Historical Strongholds of the Enemy in Your Region(s)

A. Look for historical patterns of excessive violence: mass murders, racial riots, lynching's, rapes or abductions.

B. Search for localized patterns of accidental and premature deaths.

C. Find places where numerous witchcraft sites or sacrifices have taken place. Blood sacrifices of humans and animals empower demons to demonize an area.

D. Learn the localized history of Freemasonry or Greek sorority/fraternity houses in your region or campus; this history holds a key to discovering how to redeem your city or campus.

E. Dig out the old gathering places for KKK, Odd Fellows, Shriners, etc.

F. Search for notable historic markers for confederate dead.

G. Find out if word curses have been placed on the city. If so, try to locate the exact place where they were given.

7 Ways to Discover Historical Revival Movements in Your Region(s)

A. Start out by searching for the Pentecostal movement of the 1900s.

B. Search for the Holiness movement's revivals (1800s) in tents, brush arbors or meetinghouses.

C. Uncover the paths of Methodist circuit riders; if possible find where and what they preached.

D. Look for mass gathering places for church or tent services in city squares.

E. Find out the specifics: the messages being preached, worship songs sung, types of manifestations to have occurred.

F. Learn the impacts of revival meetings: salvation, holiness, healing, unity, missions; try to discover what theme was being highlighted.

G. Discover the targeted audience: homeless, black, white, other ethnic groups, the poor, rich or even the young.

Once locating these wells and learning some of their history, the next step is to pray on- site. Gather those who have a calling and authority in the land to pray. Remember that this is not for everyone. It's important to pray with the right people at these sites. When you pray, seek Jesus specifically.

If a lot of evil has been present, then ask Jesus for specific ways to break the power of the enemy. Wait for His response. If mighty moves of God have taken place in the past there, then ask Him for heaven's blueprints for that area. See how Jesus wants to build on what was already laid. Then ask Him for some ways or practical actions that can be taken to redeem the entire land. Journal and record them. You will be surprised as to what God will reveal to you.

2. Redigging the Wells: Praying and Receiving Heaven's Blueprint for Your Region

7 Ways to Discover Blueprints for Cities and Regions

A. **Mapping out** strategic prayer points within the different communities that make up your city.

B. **Pray for** simple and thoughtful approaches to assist the poor and hurting communities; they hold a major key to unlocking your campus or region.

C. **Build** relationships with leaders. One on one is still the best approach.

D. **Hold** collaborative dinners or lunches. Gather leaders around a corporate vision and feed them. Have them share. Create space for extended prayer and answers to be revealed in these meetings. Listen to what the Spirit is saying through all of them.

E. **Serve** communion with the land on cursed sites. Take half of the bread and the cup of communion and place the other half in the ground. The bread represents Christ's body broken for us, and the cup represents His blood poured out for the remission of sins. When you do this you are breaking ancient curses and powers over the land while restoring the land's original identity and calling. Seal it by pouring anointing oil on-site. This sets apart your region unto holiness (see Isaiah 53:5; 1 Peter 2:24; Genesis 4:12; Ephesians 1:7; Numbers 35:33-34).

F. **Stake** the land. Bury stakes with Scripture and biblical declarations at the four corners of your region.

G. **Rename** the gates or the wells. Names are very important. In the Bible, God named all the gates of Israel's city and temple. Isaac also named the wells he redug. If you don't name the gates of your region the enemy will. Once you dig out these places, ask Jesus what He wants to rename your region.

3. Breaking the Well Open: Shifting the Atmosphere over Your City

7 Ways to Unlock the Wells of Revival in Your City, Campus and Region

A. **Conduct** strategic prayer walks and pick up trash along the way. Cleaning up the physical conditions of your city is an act of faith. Prophetically, this releases angelic armies to clean up the spiritual conditions of the same area.

B. **Build** extended 24/7 prayer and worship gatherings on historical sites. This can range anywhere from twenty-four hours to two hundred-plus hours. This type of ongoing worship provides many places for a variety of churches and ministries to be involved. It releases a corporate sound that has the power to overthrow a corporate stronghold.

C. Activate leaders. Gather leaders to pray on-site and declare the Word over specific prayer points over the region.

D. Bring together the spiritual and civil governments in the place of prayer. Gather these leaders together on common ground issues. Find the common enemy. Discover what specific issues plague the city, and then rally these leaders on those points. In ancient times, when a king was welcomed into a city, both the spiritual and civil authorities came together to welcome him in.

E. Mobilize the ordinances. Take foot-washing, water baptisms and communion outside the four walls. The ordinances have a specific power that can release the land from demonic strongholds. If possible, conduct meetings where these stations are activated simultaneously in the context of worship.

F. Feed the people for free. By feeding the people even the simplest of meals defensive walls are broken down, and they have a greater ability to receive what's being released. Win their hearts, and you will win their attention.

G. Give the young the platform. For explosive meetings, give the young adults and youth the platform as much as possible. This generation carries an unusual ability to usher in the presence of God. Furthermore, provide a place where these young adults can reach out to the poor and hurting of the region in the same place. By merging these two groups together (fiery young adults and the homeless and broken) you will see the power of heaven explode in your midst.